No More Monsters in the Closet

Also by Jeffrey L. Brown, M.D.

The Complete Parents' Guide to Telephone Medicine: How, When and Why to Call Your Child's Doctor

Pediatric Telephone Medicine: Principles, Triage, and Advice

No More Monsters in the Closet

*Teaching Your Children to Overcome
Everyday Fears and Phobias*

By Jeffrey L. Brown, M.D.

with Julie Davis

ℙ

Prince Paperbacks
New York

To our wonderful children,
Holly and Nicholas   —J.L.B.
Alexandra and Samuel   —J.D.

Copyright © 1995 by Jeffrey L. Brown and Canvis Group, Inc.

Published by Crown Publishers, Inc., 201 East 50th Street, New York, New York 10022. Member of the Crown Publishing Group.

Random House, Inc. New York, Toronto, London, Sydney, Auckland

Crown is a trademark of Crown Publishers, Inc.

Manufactured in the United States of America

Design by Cynthia Dunne

Library of Congress Cataloging-in-Publication Data

Brown, Jeffrey L.
    No more monsters in the closet: teaching your children to overcome
everyday fears and phobias / Jeffrey L. Brown with Julie Davis.
        1. Fear in children.   2. Child rearing.   I. Davis, Julie.   II. Title.
    BF723.F4B76 1995   94-44048
    649'.1—dc20   CIP

ISBN 0-517-88183-7

10 9 8 7 6 5 4 3 2 1
First Edition

Contents

Acknowledgments

We wish to thank Len Canter for his invaluable editorial assistance in developing this project to its fullest.

Imagination Training

What It Is, Why It Works

"My four-year-old son Eric is afraid of dogs. What can I do to help him get over it?"

As a pediatrician I'm asked about childhood fears almost as often as I'm asked about runny noses and rashes. This question came from a neighbor who stopped me at the library one Saturday afternoon. Here's what I told her.

Turn a penny into a "magic charm" by rubbing it three times on your son's elbow. (You use a penny because it's instantly replaceable should it get lost.) Next, have him go through a series of rehearsals with his magic charm. Start at a toy store where he will see stuffed toy dogs. Show him that the stuffed animals can't hurt him because he has his magic penny with him. On another day take Eric to a pet store where he can see several little puppies in cages or behind a barrier so that there is no likelihood of direct contact before he's ready. Ask him to show you his magic penny and remind him that the penny is keeping him safe. Within a week, arrange to visit a family friend whom you know has a fairly docile, well-trained dog that Eric has seen in the past. To provide him with another experience of positive reinforcement, have the dog stay on the other side of the room. Since Eric has his magic penny with him, he should feel comfortable with the dog's proximity and might even want the dog to come closer, but unless *he* feels ready, he shouldn't be forced or cajoled into actually touching the dog. Eventually, you will take him to a familiar park where you know people walk their dogs. Eric will have his magic penny with him, and since he's already tested it out in a variety of positive situations, he will have gained a sense of control over his fear and be able to enjoy the outing without panicking should a dog cross his path— even without his magic penny.

It's All in Your Imagination

Dogs make up only one of the dozens of common childhood fears and apprehensions that may affect a child at one time or another between infancy and adolescence. The technique I gave to Eric's mother is an example of what I call Imagination Training, a concept that helps you show your children how to use their own imagination to allay their fears and, in turn, develop confidence in themselves. (It can even be used to help kids get over bad habits.) Imagination Training, or "IT," can help your child to:

- cope with real or perceived fears;
- improve self-confidence and performance, at school and at play;
- relieve physical and emotional stress and distress.

Years ago, while attending lectures geared to clinical psychologists on relaxation techniques and stress control (important tools for pediatricians because they must try to relax unhappy, anxious patients every day), I realized that many of the techniques presented could have far wider applications. The concepts could be used by parents for situations faced by children in everyday life, in the same way that clinical psychologists use them to deal with more severe mental and physical problems.

Far from being technical or even complex, "IT" works by very simply switching your child's focus from the problem to its solution. "IT" offers many ways to achieve this goal, depending on the specific problem your child is facing as well as his or her age. "IT" techniques include *relaxation* to calm and soothe mind and body; *distraction* to rechannel concentration from the negative to the positive; *empowerment*, or returning a sense of control over the problem to your child (anxiety comes when the child feels that the fear is doing the controlling). And the best part is that "IT" uses every child's special mental power: imagination. Yes, fantasy play, something most kids do every day, can help kids get over their tears, fears, and even bad habits; they can feel safe in situations that make them stressed or anxious. For immediate problems such as a painful bruise or an infrequent booster shot, the emphasis is on short-term distraction. For more difficult situations such as shyness or a fear of the dark, the emphasis is on long-term coping skills that call for more elaborate solutions—elaborate in the sense of sophisticated, not complicated. Imagination Training incorporates different approaches that are age-specific, but all of its concepts have a common theme: to help your children gain some control over their lives and what is subsequently going to happen to them.

Why You and Your Child Need "IT"

You might think of your own child's fear of dogs as something he or she will outgrow, but the situation can get worse while you're waiting for that to happen. First, your whole family will find it difficult to cope with the child's anxiety level, and, second, there is the chance that the fear will intensify rather than fade, making it even harder to handle. Another tendency some parents have is to minimize or ignore the fear, hoping it will go away. But that, too, can easily backfire: If parents don't take a child's concerns seriously, his feelings of self-worth can suffer.

Even parents who decide to deal with their child's fear head-on may still find themselves in a quandary, unsure of exactly how to help the child, embarrassed at the prospect of calling their pediatrician for advice, and worried about the possibility that a child psychologist might be needed. Ironically, despite parents' apprehensions, they have the ability to help their child get through most of life's rough moments. In the same way a parent distracts a child's attention from a cut finger or from a frightening sound, the parent can help him master his fears and gain a sense of control in almost every anxiety-provoking instance. Relieving Eric's dog phobia is just one example of how Imagination Training can refine the parenting skills already developed, using simple, often familiar concepts to help the child solve a wide spectrum of specific, often frustrating, but totally normal problems. Here's why it worked so well.

Most children are intrigued by magic (it also usually requires them to use their imagination). Using a magic or good-luck charm to "ward off evil" is a familiar idea. Parents will frequently say, "Here, take this for good luck," and give their child a lucky charm or a small family heirloom such as a pin to wear or carry with them. And it's something that kids do on their own. Your sixth grader has her special good-luck pen; your high school junior has a football jersey he absolutely must wear when taking a test. Imagination Training shows you how simple ideas such as a good-luck charm can be more fully developed and used in situations that you might not have thought of, from getting over first-day-of-kindergarten jitters to overcoming a phobia.

When I suggested the lucky penny to Eric's mother, I made it more "effective" in two distinct ways. The spell of a good-luck charm is instantly broken if the charm is lost . . . unless it is a common object that your child makes "lucky" by rubbing it on his elbow three times! So I had her make Eric's good-luck charm from a replaceable penny. It could easily have been a pebble or small rock from the backyard or the neighborhood park. But above all it is an object that is always available to Eric in case he needs a new one—say he unexpectedly finds himself in the vicinity of a dog but has left the original penny at home on his dresser. Eric quickly learned that he can create a new lucky charm all by himself whenever necessary.

The second component was having Eric go through a series of rehearsals. Eric's fear developed over a period of time; giving him a number of progressive positive experiences helped him shed the fear gradually as he simultaneously gained the confidence he lacked. Although each experience brought Eric into closer contact with a real dog, his sense of control increased as well. By the time a strange dog brushed against his leg in the park, he had a wealth of positive associations to draw on. In a matter of weeks he began "reminiscing" with his mother, and as they passed a Siberian husky one day, he actually said, "Remember how I used to be afraid of dogs?" as if months had gone by!

Control: The Key Factor

One of the scariest feelings anyone, adult or child, can have is that he has no control and that things just happen by chance. But as soon as one regains some sense of power, a lot of the anxiety tends to decrease significantly. How can you regain control? By relaxing and then narrowing your focus to a single thought or idea. Calming down gives you a better perspective, and by focusing you can turn a free-floating sense of anxiety into a specific problem that needs to be addressed. You are now back in control, able to concentrate on the problem at hand and look for a solution to it.

Another element that helps a child regain control is "selective awareness," which allows him to ignore what is worrying him. It also allows him to temporarily believe that something is true even when it's not, either because it's pleasurable to him or because it helps him cope with his problem. Adults use selective awareness in certain kinds of situations just to get through the day. Take driving a car. Most of the time we think nothing of getting behind the wheel, but in the back of our minds we know that the car is really just a machine and something can go wrong with it at any time. We know there is a possibility that the brakes won't work when we step on the pedal or that another car can appear out of nowhere and hit us. We just act as if it's not going to happen. So in essence, we function at two levels: At one level there is an awareness that "bad things" can happen, and at the other level we make the decision to ignore them for the time being.

Why "IT" Works

Imagination Training in all its age-specific forms works because kids shift easily between reality and fantasy. Many adults do it, too, as when you're reading a book and suddenly feel that you are in the story—when the writer talks about the cold, you feel a chill; when a character has a parched mouth, you feel thirsty. Allowing yourself to become so immersed is a type of fantasy. Some children use fantasy as a way of getting through difficult situations. Those in very unhappy homes might try to imagine that their parents aren't fighting as their way of getting through the day. Other times, fantasy is used in a creative and fun way. If you watch children play superheroes or space warriors, you will see that while playing, they are imagining they really are those characters.

Younger children often have imaginary friends. You'll be relieved to know studies have shown that, in general, children with imaginary friends grow up to be more secure than those who don't. Having imaginary friends is actually a good sign of healthy psychological development! The trouble with imaginary friends is that kids sometimes demand that the friend be included in *every* activity. It's okay for you to "participate" just as long as it doesn't become disruptive to your entire household. As kids get older they engage in different fantasy play. Young teenagers are notorious for fantasizing about everything from love affairs with rock stars to becoming nuclear physicists, and they can make up an entire fantasy world for themselves.

One of the objections to kids watching television is that it is a passive experience and they don't get to use their minds. But, kids are often engaged in fantasy play while they watch, and it may not be all passive to them. They are so totally immersed in the story, you could bring a bathtub into the living room and bathe them, and they wouldn't even notice you were with them. Whether kids do it to be protective, or creative, or just for fun, their ability to switch back and forth between reality and fantasy makes them particularly receptive to Imagination Training.

Imagination Training Grows Up with Your Child

How To Adapt the Techniques to Your Child's Age

WHEN A NEWBORN CRIES, parents wish for the day she can communicate her needs with words. When a toddler doesn't understand why he must get a shot, parents wonder how many years it will be before they can use rational explanations. With Imagination Training, however, there is an effective approach that can be used at any age. The objectives as well as the specific techniques do change with your child's age: For infants and small children, "IT" is used for calming; for preschoolers, physical and emotional stress can be relieved; for older children, "IT" addresses more complex problems, such as self-confidence. There will be some overlaps; the pace at which your child develops will be different from the child next door, but the following descriptions show how the techniques you use will change to keep up with your child as he or she gets older, more verbal, and more sophisticated. Included are some of the most effective Imagination Training solutions for each age group.

The Preverbal Years, Up to Age Two

Because they don't understand complex directions, infants and toddlers up to twenty-four months respond best to nonverbal techniques. The most effective of these is motion—any repetitive motion that tends to have a calming effect, such as rocking, stroking, and holding. That's why baby swings are so soothing and why children fall asleep so readily in the car. Hand-holding or stroking a hand for the older children in this age group tends to have a hypnotic quality and is relaxing. So do certain sounds—think about how your baby reacts to the sound of the vacuum cleaner or clothes dryer. A baby will quickly respond to your whispering in his ear, humming, or singing a simple tune. The melody will soon become very familiar to him: Hearing the song will be both soothing when he is upset and distracting when you want to shift his attention away from an imminent shot.

Other distraction techniques for this age group are very simple and direct. Bubble blowing, music boxes, and wind-up toys get their attention immediately. Or hold up a favorite toy or an object that tends to gain the attention of your child and say firmly, "Look at this!" One- and two-year-olds will respond to visually appealing storybooks or boardbooks with simple photographs. Simply open the book, point to a colorful picture, and tell baby what it is. In a pinch, just making and maintaining eye contact will do.

The Early Verbal Years, Ages Two to Four

Many Imagination Training techniques for this age group are similar to those used for the preverbal group but will become more engaging as your toddler matures. Where you could distract an infant with a simple toy, now you will use objects with a more complex motion, such as a mobile. Before, you were the active participant and your baby was relatively passive; now you can get your toddler to participate actively in a verbal way. For instance, when you use a picture book as a distraction, you will open it to a colorful page and ask simple questions to engage him in the distraction process: "What is this called? Does the bunny have a name? Where is he hopping to?" If you show your child a pop-up book, you can ask questions about what's going on in the story. If you're using bubble blowing as the distraction, let your toddler do the blowing.

The language that you use with a preschooler must remain very directed. "I'm going to kiss this to make it better" or "Let me rub your boo-boo." Even the youngest kids understand that. At the dentist's office, which will look totally unfamiliar and can seem very frightening on a first visit, you might say, "This might seem scary, but I'm going to hold your hand so nothing can hurt you." Saying such very directed things has two effects: It's reassuring, and it distracts your child from his thoughts of discomfort by shifting his focus to you. When a two-year-old shies away from a dog, you can directly say, "I'll be with you so it can't hurt you. Let's go near this doggie because it won't hurt you. Some doggies can, but most doggies won't." In a stressful situation, that is about the extent of any "discussion" you should have with kids in this age group. In general, the younger the child, the shorter your discussion should be.

Toddlers continue to respond to singing and humming, and the more verbal they get, the more they will sing along. The classic "Whistle While You Work" from *Snow White and the Seven Dwarfs* was my son's special "afraid of bugs" song. At first we sang it together; soon he was able to recognize it as something he could sing or hum on his own whenever an errant fly or spider came into view. If your child is fond of a particular song, tell him that's the one you'll both hum or sing in scary situations. Also consider the lyrics from *The King and I* and have your child "whistle a happy tune whenever he feels afraid." Another great idea is to make up your own words that are appropriate to your child's particular fear and to whatever change in circumstances will make him or her feel happy again; devise your own melody or rewrite the lyrics to one he or she already knows.

One "relaxation" technique that works for some kids in this age group, but is somewhat unnerving for adults, is to allow them to scream out their anxiety—a great distraction/focusing technique. Tell your child to yell as loud as he can to let out all his fears—one time only. Repeat performances are only with permission.

In a pinch, three- and four-year-olds can tune out by chewing gum (sugarless, of course); explain that with each chew he or she will feel happier and more relaxed. Even before they can do it on their own, kids are fascinated by the dynamics of bubble gum; your blowing gum bubbles for them will be a great distraction. You will soon see that almost any distraction can be used to calm a worried child.

The Early School Years, Ages Four to Six

This is the age when techniques based more on Imagination Training come into play, when children start to respond to concepts like the magic charm. They are also old enough now to attempt true, albeit basic, relaxation techniques. You can teach some five- and six-year-olds to do deep breathing when they feel uncomfortable. If they're able to count, you can have them count to three as they take each breath and explain to them that with every "breathing out" they are going to feel more and more relaxed.

Another simple relaxation exercise they can attempt is to focus all their attention on a body part. An easy one is a thumbnail. Take a fine-point marker and draw a happy face right on your child's thumbnail. Have your child stare at it and try not to think about anything else. You might add deep breathing as a second calming element. Use the right words to start your child off: "Let's do some breathing exercises. You'll be surprised to see what happens next." To demonstrate what relaxation means, ask your child to tense a muscle or make the tightest fist she can muster, then release it, and point out how much nicer it feels when it is relaxed.

The next concept they will be able to grasp is picturing and concentrating on a happy thought. You can initiate this with a simple suggestion: "Think of one thing or one place that makes you happy." Then follow it up by saying, "Tell me about it." Examples include a birthday party, a family trip, and having a pet. Ask the child who wants a puppy to imagine the puppy in her mind and help her to "see" it running around and to see herself petting it. Start the fantasy by saying, "Let's pretend that . . ." or "Let's make believe that . . ." Practice this every day. Some children will be able to do this with their eyes closed; most will prefer to keep theirs open. Either way, let your child know he can recall this happy picture any time he wants to feel good.

If imaginative play isn't your child's strong suit (or if you feel more comfortable starting with something simpler), just counting can be very relaxing. You might choose the proverbial sheep or numbers on an imaginary blackboard written with her favorite color of imaginary chalk.

The Middle Years, Ages Seven to Twelve

You can now start to get into more sophisticated imagery with more detailed and personalized fantasies. What stays constant is the message that the Imagination Training exercise gives to your child. That he or she

- is in control;
- is safe—nothing can hurt him or her;
- can go anywhere and do anything that he or she wants to do.

The only thing that varies is the specific image or series of images you choose, determined solely by what appeals to your particular child.

Some children at this age become fascinated with dinosaurs. A great imagination setting would be a Jurassic park. Have your son imagine that he's in a giant park filled with dinosaurs except that he has control over them; he can jump on the back of any dinosaur he likes, and that dinosaur will take him wherever he wants to go in the park. Help him see that he's in control: While he's sitting on one dinosaur, none of the others can see him. He can ride up to any animal and look it over as closely as he wants. To draw him into the fantasy, you might ask him to describe all the sizes, shapes, and colors of the dinosaurs in the park.

Girls are often fascinated by mermaids. Your daughter might like to imagine being in a colony with other mermaids, maybe even being their queen. If she has more of an independent personality, let her imagine that she has the ocean to herself and can swim anywhere in the sea that she wants to. Because of her long fishtail, she can swim faster than anyone else, and nobody can ever hurt her.

A special note to parents on the gender issue underlying these choices. No one is sure if it's environmental or intrinsic, but many boys seem to gravitate toward dinosaurs simply and naturally, and many girls, to mermaids. We chose these particular examples of themes because it makes sense to offer children the images they most respond to.

As children get closer to age ten, they often become interested in mechanical things. For instance, if your child is computer-literate and loves to play computer games, an appropriate distraction technique is to have him imagine his computer game in his mind: He can imagine moving the cursor or controlling the hero by moving him from one box to another to achieve a higher score. Simpler games work, too, from word jumbles to beginner math problems, even recalling a series of riddles.

If you are unsure of your child's current likes, do what a doctor or therapist might do before trying to fix on a specific image: Sit down with your child and ask these introductory questions. What kinds of imagination things do you like to do? What kinds of sports do you like to play? Would you rather play by yourself or with others? What kinds of things make you happy? What kinds of things make you frightened? Don't feel embarrassed that you have to ask. Kids' tastes change all the time, and parents are often the last to know what is out in her group of friends and what is in. Remember, you're still way ahead of the professionals because you already have an established relationship with your children, making it easy for them to communicate their likes and dislikes. (And most kids will be thrilled that you cared enough to ask them.)

Some parents will find it helpful to draw up a list of things that make their kids happy and create a script of potential imagery themes. If your child is sports-oriented, good possibilities include playing in a baseball or soccer game and swimming. If your child plays competitive sports, he or she can imagine any of the strokes or other moves necessary to performing that particular sport, always with the premise that in the fantasy he or she is really terrific at it. You will help evoke every aspect of the sport, incorporating as much sensory information as possible. The "fine points" of an imagined horseback ride, for instance, would start with a description of the horse. What color is it? How big is it? What does it smell like? What does it feel like to sit on? What do its hooves sound like as they hit the ground? Is the leather saddle smooth? Do you ever brush the horse before you get on it? Basically, you're trying to draw on as many senses as you can to engage the child in the imagery. You will also want to use as much descriptive language as you can: light as a feather, heavy as lead, sweet as sugar, cold as ice—phrases that carry an image.

The Teen Years, Ages Thirteen to Eighteen

The real difference between seven- to twelve-year-olds and teenagers is not so much a change in interests—though both sexes become more interested in music, sports, and clothes, and their TV attention makes a noticeable shift to the soaps!—as a further deepening in sophistication of the imagery you help them create. For example, the seven-year-old little leaguer's image of playing baseball is simplistic: "Someone is hitting a ball to you, and you're running for it. You're going to catch it. Wow! There it is in your glove. That's great! You did it." When you're talking to a teenager, you need to create a more sophisticated atmosphere, rich with details and sensory images: "Here you go, sliding into the base. See the dust coming up around you. Feel your foot touch the bag. You can feel the tag: It's late; you're safe. And the fans are cheering in the stands." Even though you're still talking about baseball, the kind of imagery you're using has changed to adapt to the age of the child.

Yes, You and Your Child Can Do It

By now you're probably wondering how you can do this on your own and how you can possibly convince your anxious child to give it a try. Let me talk about kids first. I've already discussed their affinity for fantasy play. Building on that, I have found, both in my own practice and in my investigations of various techniques used by psychologists and other practitioners, that kids are not only receptive to trying something new to help them conquer their fears or problems but they are also extremely successful at learning and benefiting from these techniques.

I'd like to tell you about a ten-year-old boy named Eddie, his skeptical parents, and the very simple demonstration I did for them in my office. I asked Eddie to hold out his hands and imagine that they were magnets and were going to get pulled together. I said, "Watch what I am showing you. You will find this very interesting. There's a switch in your brain that turns up the electricity that makes the magnets draw closer together. I want you to turn it up a little bit. Now a little bit more. And a little bit more." As I was talking, Eddie's hands came together. The look on his parents' faces said, "Holy cow! How'd you do that?" I simply explained to them and to Eddie that imagination can affect the body and that imagining your hands are magnets is just one of many things you can accomplish. We then went on to discuss the problem that Eddie was having and ways we could try to solve it.

You might be unsure about your own ability to help your child with Imagination Training concepts, particularly once your son or daughter becomes verbal and distraction techniques call for more than holding up a toy or singing a lullaby. But the truth is, you *can* learn to do this; in fact, many parents have instinctively been doing some form of it all along.

Some parents are very creative; for them, even the most

advanced "IT" techniques will come very naturally. Others will benefit from having a list of things to do, a kind of cookbook with lots of variations to account for the wide range of differences in children. Just as some people are "born salespeople" and learn selling techniques very easily, others need to be, and can be, taught all the essentials. I'm going to furnish you with many choices for dealing with every topic covered in this book, with multiple suggestions for each age group. This will help parents to whom it may not come naturally as well as show other parents how to use Imagination Training in situations they might not have already considered.

Even though "IT" provides many options for every problem, including dialogue you can use word for word, I know from my own pediatric practice that there are parents who believe they aren't imaginative enough (or at all), who insist they won't know what to do or who feel awkward about trying this. But I want to assure you that you *can* do it, that you *will* be able to find the right tone of voice, the right words and the right body language to help you develop the kind of rapport with your child that's going to make this work.

First, you have to develop within yourself the feeling that you really can help your child. And if you think about it, you'll realize that deep down you already know it's true. All you have to do is look back through past experiences with your child; think of the times she was afraid and you were able to calm her. Look at the way you've been parenting up until now; think about all the things you felt insecure about in the beginning, things that in retrospect seem so simple: Is my baby getting enough to eat? How often should I change his diaper? Am I holding her the right way? You gradually developed the necessary skills and after a time didn't have to think twice about them. Realize that the same thing will happen with Imagination Training. It will soon become second nature.

Prevailing wisdom these days says that parents shouldn't feel nervous, but I always tell them that being upset or nervous for your child is okay. When a new mother feels as though she's being stabbed through the heart every time her infant cries, all that means is that she loves her child and is feeling empathy; it doesn't have any "deeper" meaning than that. The fact that a parent has self-doubt and insecurity isn't necessarily bad. These are actually indicative of the parent's love for the child and the desire to help that child in the best way possible. But, you mustn't let these natural feelings overwhelm you to the point where you're afraid to try something that might help your child.

When you're searching for the "right way" to communicate any of the ideas in this book, first remember that you want to be able to give your children a feeling of love and the assurance that what you're going to tell them will help them. When your children accept you as a figure of trust and as a figure of love, they are more likely to accept the things you are telling them.

Your children will be willing to test Imagination Training ideas if you present them in a way they find acceptable; how you do that will depend on their age. With younger children you have to be more concrete in the way you talk. You can say, "Rub this on your elbow three times, and it will bring you good luck." But if you're talking to an older child and you know there's a good chance that her response will be, "Gee, this is really baloney," then your approach might be something like, "Let's see what happens if we do this" or "I heard that this is a great idea. I'm not sure why rubbing this penny on your elbow is going to help you, but I heard that it really works well." (For the older child, telling her to hold the penny in a fist until it's warm might be more appealing.)

Generally this shift in approach is needed after age five or six, but it can be difficult to make generalizations. There will be some clever four-year-olds with whom the concrete approach won't work and some seven-year-olds who will still accept it. You will need to do a little experimenting on your own. Very often you can be more firm and direct in panic-type situations: The more afraid a child is, the more he wants you to tell him what to do and the more likely he is to listen. It is in these situations that doctors are best able to introduce Imagination Training techniques to their patients. If a child is absolutely panicked, a pediatrician can say, "Do just what I tell you, and you'll be okay." If it's not a panic situation but instead part of a discussion, then what usually works best is talking in terms of "Let's see what happens if we try X, Y, and Z." Sometimes parents have a very hard time doing this, but there are situations that demand it, such as when you must give your child medicine. Take a look at Chapter 8 for dealing with this and other "nonnegotiables."

From a practical point of view, it's important to use *age-appropriate language* so that your discussion won't go right over your child's head. If you're unsure of what is appropriate, take a look at the language used in books designed for your child's age group; your local librarian or your child's teacher can be a great help, steering you to the right choices. Also, talking at your child's *eye level* is very important. A younger child can see you eye to eye when sitting on your lap and facing you; you can achieve this equal footing with an older child if you sit while he stands or if you both recline on a rug, propped up on your elbows.

Speak in a way that's loving but that also sounds *self-assured;* if you're hesitant, your child will doubt you, and the idea you're trying to get across won't take hold. When you sound confident, your child will be more likely to believe what you're telling her. Also, use a tone of voice and set an atmosphere that you have found to be *calming* in the past. For example, in your family does a one-on-one discussion work better than discussing topics at the dinner table? Is bedtime a more receptive time than after school when your child might still be wound up with energy?

Finally, mix in a measured amount of *authority* with your sense of self-assurance. It gives the message "I've been through this in the past, and I really know how to help you. If you try what I tell you, things are going to come out okay." And you know what? They will.

G.R.E.A.T.
The Five Steps of Imagination Training

An easy way to be certain you integrate the major components of Imagination Training in your approach is to establish each of these five steps.

G. is for GOAL. Decide on the objective—what your child wants to accomplish or what outcome he or she is looking for. You ask, "What would you like to have happen?"

R. is for REFOCUS. Have your child focus on your voice (or an object or core concept from Chapter 3) instead of on his problem. You say, "Listen to me carefully. I can help you."

E. is for EXPLANATION. Outline what you're going to propose. You say, "This is what we're going to do . . ."

A. is for ACTION. Now you get your child to participate. This is actually the double action of your child's stopping the undesirable behavior and starting to regain control of the situation. You say, "What is your favorite place? Tell me all about it."

T. is for TRAINING. Reinforce the Imagination Training exercise by practicing it at times when the behavior isn't actually happening. This reinforcement through rehearsals instills confidence. And add a measure of praise. You say, "You are doing great. Keep going."

The Dynamics of Distraction

The Core Concepts of Imagination Training

TO GIVE YOU AN idea of the variety of choices that Imagination Training offers, here are four different techniques for dealing with a specific childhood fear, needlephobia, one of the most prevalent causes of panic in a doctor's office. These suggestions are geared to those in the four- to eight-year-old range who are familiar with shots and who get fearful in advance of the office visit (many times successful approaches will overlap the age categories). These "IT" techniques apply to the routine "finger prick" blood test in which blood is taken from a fingertip rather than a vein in the arm, although the concepts can certainly be adapted to all procedures involving a needle, including injections. (For more on this topic, see Chapter 7.)

Bear in mind as you read through these that there is no single "right" way to overcome a fear of needles, or any fear, for that matter. The best approach is the one that works for your child. You may become comfortable with one of the following, then find it doesn't work all the time or one day find that it has outlived its usefulness. Depending on the specifics of your child's fear, one answer might be more appropriate than the others. The more choices you have, the better prepared you are to help your child. Those unsure of themselves can offer these word-for-word; otherwise, feel free to adapt them as needed.

1. The Magic Glove

Like the lucky penny, the Magic Glove has the power to shield the child who wears it from discomfort; the key difference is that the Magic Glove is invisible. You are going to help your child imagine it, first by thinking it, then by seeing it, and last by feeling it. Here's what you might say: "I want you to imagine a glove that can be put over your hand to make it sleepy and numb. Let me help you do this. See the glove? What color is it? It looks as though it will fit your hand perfectly. Can you count all five of its fingers?" Asking a lot of questions draws your child into the imagery. "Now we're going to pull it over your hand very, very slowly. Feel each finger going into the glove. Now each finger is snug inside the glove. The glove is getting tighter. Do you feel it? That's good because when it starts to feel real tight over your hand, then nothing can hurt your hand."

The imagery distracts your child's attention from the needle while your voice relaxes him and eases his anxiety. This technique works best when you can have practice sessions before going to the doctor's office. You can even poke his index finger with the blunt end of a pin; many children won't even feel it. But rather than presenting it as a preparation for a needle (kids don't need to be told about a routine office visit until the day before or even the morning of the visit), it is best to introduce it as a game.

The Magic Glove requires imagination, and some kids in this age group just won't be ready for it. It also takes a few minutes more in the doctor's office, and, frankly, sometimes your doctor or the nurse might not be willing to participate. In either case, the Magic Swab is a quick alternative.

2. The Magic Swab

In this distraction you ask your child to imagine that the alcohol used to clean her finger is going to make it numb. "I heard that the doctor [or nurse] is using a special medicine. It's different from the one they used before, and if it is rubbed on your fingertip five times, the needle won't hurt you." Again, practice this at home. Go through the ritual of swabbing the finger with a water-soaked cotton ball or swab. (Though you might have rubbing alcohol to use at home, it's better to preserve the mystique of the doctor's "special medicine.") At the doctor's office simply ask your practitioner to swab the area five times while you count them off.

3. Distraction Action

A different approach is to shift your child's attention away from the needle completely. The simplest way to do this is to exert pressure with two of your fingertips on one of your child's shoulders. Explain what you will be doing this way: "As soon as the doctor starts to clean your finger, I'm going to press right here on your shoulder. The more I press, the farther down your arm you're going to feel the pressing, all the way down to your hand. You tell me when that starts to happen because when it does, you will hardly feel anything the doctor does." Start pressing when the nurse or doctor swabs the fingertip; it will take only those few seconds for you to apply shoulder pressure and "talk" it down to your child's hand. Just as you press you can add, "I'm going to start to push now. Feel me holding your shoulder tighter and tighter. Feel it go down your arm to your elbow. Now it's pushing down your forearm. Can you feel it at your wrist? Now it's spreading to each of your fingers." If your child says she can't feel the sensation farther down her arm, say, "Great! That means it'll hurt you even less!" In the time it takes to guide her imagination to her fingertips, the doctor will most likely be finished.

4. Aroma Therapy

Sometimes it's the smell of the alcohol rather than the actual needle that brings on a child's fear; and kids come to associate the smell with pain. If you can get them past the alcohol part, then the needle won't bother them so much. First, you need to pick a scent substitute that appeals to your child. Then you can help him imagine that he smells it. If he loves the fragrance of flowers, you may have him imagine that he is walking through a field of flowers where he picks up a pretty pink rose and brings it up to his nose to inhale. If it is the aroma of freshly baked chocolate chip cookies that he adores, help him imagine seeing a plate of still-warm cookies, picking one up, and breaking it in half to release its chocolaty steam. Again, the more questions you ask to help him visualize the image— How big is the cookie? Is it too hot to bite into? Are the chips light or dark brown? Have they all melted?—the more real it will seem. And, of course, little girls who love to wear Mom's perfume may be distracted by a squirt of the real thing from a purse atomizer.

Needlephobia is just one of many fears that respond to distraction techniques. In the following chapters you'll find distractions like those described above that have very specific applications. You will find others that have extremely wide applications, that will work in many different situations. An example is blowing out the candles on an imaginary birthday cake. This one spans many age groups, and you can use it virtually anytime your child is upset. It is simplicity itself: You or your child holds up the fingers of one hand (two, if you like) to simulate the candles on a birthday cake. (Having him use his own hand has the advantage of teaching him to do it in the future on his own should the need arise—say, if a bad scrape brings him to the nurse's station at school and he's panicked without you.) Now your child blows on the fingers all at once or, better yet, individually. You can suggest to your child that he take relaxing deep breaths in between blows. Or you can suggest that the candles are hot and that heat causes pain, but as each one is blown out, the pain becomes less. You can elaborate on the cake distraction by incorporating it into a whole birthday party, reliving one that you know was an especially happy time or spinning the tale of a fantasy party, with a theme he'd like for his next birthday.

Another example of an engaging fantasy-play distraction is taking imaginary lessons; even a three-year-old can imagine learning to drive a car, fly a plane, or ride a horse. Or ask your child to tell you all about a favorite toy, game, or story. Retelling the story of a favorite video or describing the action of a favorite computer game is very absorbing, and the more detail you ask for, the harder your child will work at it and the more she will be distracted. To have your child recount a treasured book, help her imagine turning each page, and ask each time what comes next. Don't worry about this being too hard: When it comes to favorite books, kids have an amazing memory, often being able to recite the story verbatim well before being able to read the words.

Other distracting "retellings" can be of special trips, such as a visit to a relative in a faraway city, to the zoo, or to a park or playground on the other side of town. Embroider the reminiscence by asking questions about what she wore that day, how you traveled to the destination, and what interesting things you passed along the way. Recounting a concrete (and happy) event is an excellent technique for the child who hasn't yet developed strong imagination skills; he needs only to call on his own memory. On the other hand, the imaginative child is often able to weave a brand-new story for you if you ask a question as simple as "What would you like to do more than anything else in the world?" or "Did you see anything yesterday that you would have liked to take a picture of?"

When you're looking for distractions for the younger child to focus on, you can have him stare at a part of his body such as his foot, a crack in the wall, or even a pencil. And if he isn't interested in any handy objects, your own voice can become the focal point. Whispering will make a child try harder to listen and has a conspiratorial quality that might capture his attention. Other sounds to focus on include music and sounds in the room and on the street. Counting also works well with younger kids. Count fingers, pictures on a wall, or stairs; add a second dimension by counting colored objects such as blocks or beads that you can carry with you. The distraction can be visual, auditory, or even tactile, such as touching different textures—from the nubby upholstery on a chair to the smooth wood of a table.

To further widen the scope of possible ideas for kids of all ages,

I've included a special chapter (11) that lists suggested fantasy themes, activities, and characters from which you and your child can develop a repertoire to draw on, such as Babar and Curious George. (The books and films these characters are taken from can also provide you with age-appropriate language to use.) But rather than a closed-end list, think of it as a springboard for even more ideas: The great thing about Imagination Training is its infinite choice of subjects defined only by the specific likes and interests of your child. On the other hand, don't be afraid to use the same image or technique over and over again if it is successful.

Core Concepts for Coping

Many of the techniques I've described above involve easing a transient fear or momentary discomfort. More serious situations— like coping with daily injections for diabetes, overcoming a fear of poor school performance, or correcting a problem like social awkwardness—respond to more developed concepts such as the Takealong Friend, who can stand invisibly by your child's side and protect him, and the Pinkie Pain Switch, the one in your child's little finger that can turn off the anguish of a daily insulin shot. These core concepts are used in many forms throughout this book.

1. The Finger Circle

Your third grader has a terrifying fear of being called up to the blackboard in school. It has nothing to do with aptitude; he's just afraid of standing out in front of all his classmates. You can teach him the confidence-boosting Finger Circle with this explanation: "When I was your age, I had an uncle who taught this to me. I'm still not sure exactly how it works, but this is what my uncle thought: 'Everybody has energy that leaves their body. If you touch your cheek, you'll feel that it's warm, because the energy inside your body is leaving. But if you put your thumb and index finger together to form a circle, then the energy travels in the circle, doesn't leave your body, and instead makes you stronger. Just pinch those two fingers together; pinch them tight so that none of the energy can escape but can cycle back up your arm, making you stronger. Then you'll be able to do things you think you can't do.' "

This explanation is worded to "sound right" to the more skeptical child. With kids who are accepting of just about anything you tell them, you can be more matter-of-fact. No lengthy explanation needed. In reality, what we have done is to give the child a good-luck charm that he can create anytime it is needed.

2. The Takealong Friend

This technique is similar to yet more powerful than the Finger Circle because it capitalizes on a child's affinity for imaginary friends. A likely candidate is a superhero or -heroine; once a child reaches school age, there is sure to be at least one such character he admires. The idea is not for your child to carry around a Superman or Batman doll, but rather to *imagine* that the "real" character is standing beside him. Having a Takealong Friend is useful for overcoming separation anxiety, for example, or in situations that are perceived by a child as potentially dangerous. The Takealong Friend can also be used at home if your child is afraid of falling asleep at night or gets upset when you leave him with a baby-sitter.

This type of imaginary friend works best when the child is already a fan. He knows all of the powers that his particular hero has and that he's somebody who protects good guys and fights against evil. Explain to your child: "When I'm not around, your Takealong Hero will be keeping his eye on you, and you know that he's not going to let anything bad happen to you. So when you walk into your classroom, I want you to imagine that he is with you and is going to protect you."

Some parents prefer to stay away from commercial "Saturday morning cartoon characters," choosing instead someone they consider to have more worth. And in some cases, a religious image might be chosen. If your child is imaginative, together you can create your own character. Always go into specific detail: What is his or her name? What color is his or her hair, eyes, and costume? What are his or her good qualities? The more your child can conceptualize the image, the more real it becomes. Many youngsters respond to the friendly characters popularized on PBS. I have yet to find a three-year-old who hasn't fallen in love with Barney the Dinosaur; if your child understands his messages of love, friendship, and caring, he'd be an excellent character to use. For older kids the Takealong Friend can be a real personality your child admires, such as a sports figure or an actor, as long as you can weave the person into a story that communicates the message that this particular person is going to protect him or her.

3. "Magic Carpet," "Cloud Copter," "Pillow Palace," and Other Escapes

For some kids who feel anxious, nervous, or upset, relief comes not from the excitement of a birthday party but rather from an escape. They might want to imagine that they are flying like a bird and can take any path they like, away from whatever is bothering them. Or they might sit on a little area rug on the floor in their room (a towel makes a fine substitute) and imagine that the rug is able to fly in a magic kind of way. You can have your child fly in almost anything. A Cloud Copter is the vehicle of choice if you happen to be outside when you're discussing your child's concerns. Have her look up at the clouds and say to her, "Let's turn that cloud into a helicopter." This is a perfect example of how you can take things that are around you and use them for the specific imagery you need.

Do remember to make sure before you suggest a ride in a Cloud Copter or on a Magic Carpet or even on her own hobby horse that your child isn't afraid of heights because obviously that would defeat the purpose of the exercise! Even if a fear of heights doesn't seem to be a problem, have your child practice her flying—have her "raise off the ground" a little bit until she feels comfortable. Have her hold on to both sides of her chosen "vehicle" so that she feels secure, and let her know that she can't possibly fall off. For some children you must take away all the potential dangers: Explain that it can't crash and that a magic strap holds her in place. It will go only as fast as she wants; it will go high only if she wants it to; and it has special detectors so it can't bump into anything. There must always be a built-in element of safety.

There are other "escapes" from anxiety that don't require any travel. Help your child create a soft, safe, reassuring place like the imaginary Pillow Palace, a fantasy castle that cushions her against all anxiety with pillows in every shape, size, and color.

4. The Pinkie Pain Switch

This technique shows kids how they can gain control on their own in situations where pain and/or anxiety are present. The answer is literally at one's fingertip. Say, "Hold the lower part of one of your pinkie fingers with the opposite hand. Bend the fingertip like a switch. When the 'switch' is down, you can't feel any pain." When your daughter bruises a knee and becomes even more fearful as you try to clean it, she can flick the Pinkie Pain Switch and turn off the sting. When your son needs to have a sprained ankle wrapped and won't let the doctor touch it, he can flick the switch and turn off his apprehensions along with his discomfort.

A better-known variation of this is hand-squeezing. A child can squeeze any fears that he has into another person's hand—Mom's, Dad's, even a nurse's. The harder he squeezes, the more nervousness or pain runs out of his body. You can liken this to turning on a faucet: The more you open it, the more water flows out. If there isn't a hand to squeeze, he can squeeze the edge of a table and make his fears run out across the table and down the table legs to the floor. Or he can push down hard on the floor with one foot; the harder he pushes, the closer his foot comes to the floor, the more "bad stuff" can run out of his body. A child can also squeeze all his pain or anxiety into his own fist, then open the hand, finger by finger, to let it all out.

Putting Imagination Training to Work

The images and ideas of Imagination Training are designed to amuse and appeal to kids, but even more important are the basic underlying principles they all share: returning a sense of control to your child and giving him or her the confidence to solve the problem he or she is facing.

Each of the following chapters addresses a specific group of related problems and behaviors, from school jitters to social fears. Included in each is a description of the problem and how Imagination Training techniques work to correct it. The information provided will help you to understand the problem and discover the best solutions for your child. In each instance you will find a wealth of solutions, not just for each problem but also for each of the age groups. And to help you help your child visualize the key concepts in each chapter, line drawings make the ideas come alive.

You will probably want to turn immediately to the subject that your child is having difficulty with at this moment. It would be best, however, to take the time to read through all the chapters because virtually every guided image, every distraction tool, every fantasy play, can be adapted to fit your child's needs and help him or her master every moment of childhood.

The Elements of Successful Imagination Training

1. CONTROL. Your child can make the Cloud Copter go anywhere he wants, as fast as he wants.

2. SAFETY. The place your child goes or the imaginary vehicle he uses to get there should always have a built-in safety factor. In the Cloud Copter, for instance, the child can hold on to the "steering wheel" and fly as slowly or as low to the ground as she wants.

3. RELAXATION. The more he flies in his Cloud Copter, the more happy and relaxed he will be.

4. REWARD. The more she relaxes, the better she will feel.

Social Insecurity

Understanding and Allaying Shyness

HOW OFTEN HAVE YOU experienced this scene? Guests enter your home, and you call the children to come out and greet them. The kids appear and approach cautiously and hesitantly. You admonish them with "What's the matter? You remember Uncle Jay, don't you?" or "You know Mommy's best friend, Amy." But the kids just stare as though your friends were visitors from outer space. Despite the fact that these are people with familiar faces and who bear an indisputable safety quotient, one kid assumes a defensive posture, peering out from behind Dad's leg and avoiding eye contact, while the other mumbles something that you translate as hello. The children may then retreat for a while, but curiously two hours later they are using Uncle Jay as a trampoline and asking Amy when she can come back to play!

Parents frequently have a misconception about childhood shyness, mislabeling the natural, normal apprehension many kids demonstrate when faced with the unfamiliar. Surprising as it may sound, a certain amount of shyness is normal and helps children adjust to new surroundings.

At an adult cocktail party, two out of every ten people in attendance will be making the rounds in an aggressive fashion: "Hi, I'm Vic. It's really nice to meet you!" Two others will be standing off to the side hoping that no one notices them, and the rest of the group will move cautiously, warming up slowly and finally mixing in. Though most parents think that all kids should be outgoing socially and might even refer to their kids' bouts of shyness as a phase to be outgrown, the truth is their behavior closely mirrors that of our cocktail party guests. Switch that scene to a fourth grader's birthday party, and you'll find that the kids exhibit pretty much the same personality profiles that adults do: Some are gregarious, some are shy, and some fall somewhere in between.

It's important to recognize that a wide variety of behavior is normal. Unfortunately, if a child starts out with an initial caution when dealing with people outside his immediate family or if he happens to fall into the truly shy group (and it seems that there is a very strong hereditary disposition toward shyness), parents tend to think of the behavior as abnormal. But in most circumstances, far from being abnormal, this is simply a facet of his personality.

Another caution: It's important to neither minimize a child's apprehensions nor make too much of them. It's appropriate for you to be supportive, but be careful not to allow a fear or fears to become attention-getting behavior. Children may begin with a real fear but soon learn that they can capitalize on it. Overplaying an easily resolvable situation can effectively increase the fears they seem to have. Your goal is not necessarily to have your child acknowledge a weakness, but to inform her that this fear will probably end at some finite point.

A better way to gauge whether there's a real problem is to use your instincts to determine if your child is happy or not—whether he's uncomfortable about his social self or whether you're the one the behavior bothers. Not everybody is happy when socializing. Some adults are loners, not because of any social insecurity, but because they are simply content when off alone reading or hiking or listening to music. They are perfectly capable of good social interaction but choose to do otherwise. What your child needs is your acceptance, not pressure to conform to what you'd like. If you sense, however, that your child is unhappy because she wants to interact but can't, then some intervention on your part may be warranted.

Say Good-bye to Shy

Where to begin? Start by talking to your kids. They are often very helpful in diagnosing what's bothering them and can come up with some creative solutions. To initiate a conversation, ask a question that gets your child to focus on the problem and understand it better. You might say, "You seem to get nervous whenever it's time to stay over at Grandma's house. What part of being there worries you?" Your child might tell you things you've never considered, and once you understand the root of the problem, you can find solutions through further give-and-take. Offer suggestions, but in a nondictatorial way. Instead of "Do this . . ." say, "Why not try this . . . I think it will help." To use Imagination Training, have your child travel to Grandma's house in his Cloud Copter (as discussed in Chapter 3). Describe the journey as he flies through the air in command of the copter, his arrival marked by Grandma's comforting greeting, his unpacking favorite toys and books in the guest room or den, and all the great things Grandma has planned. Next, get his participation by having him describe being there and going through what he's apprehensive about. Finally, arm him with a relaxation technique he can use after he gets there, such as the Takealong Friend whom Grandma wouldn't mind having over as well.

There are a number of effective ways to help the truly shy kid who's unhappy about his shyness. The first rule, especially for younger children, is to start by acknowledging the child's concern, not trivializing or minimizing it. The worst strategy is to say, "Don't be silly. You'll be fine at Robby's party." As soon as you say that, you have effectively shut off any further discussion. A better strategy is to immediately acknowledge the child's concern with a more caring response such as, "I'm sorry to hear about this problem because I know that it doesn't feel good when you're feeling shy. Let's see what we can think of to help." This empathetic introduction can be bridged further with "You know what? You have a lot of good things going for you, and I bet a lot of your friends are feeling shy about going to parties, too. Maybe if we can figure out what's not fun about going, we can find ways to make it better."

For older children with a more sophisticated thought process, "What do *you* think will help?" with the emphasis on *you*, can often elicit a startling response. Kids who appear stymied by their predicament may still have their own ideas and solutions; they may just need a little encouragement to voice and explore them. If your child can't readily think of anything specific, help her recall a similar past experience and remind her of a strategy she successfully used before. Say, "Remember Megan's party over the summer? Let's try to remember what you did there to have a good time. Let's start at the beginning, when you first walked in." Use that as a jumping-off point and build from there.

This technique works not only for isolated occasions but also for most instances of "joining in." Children often have apprehensions about joining in activities that we think of as fun. But whether it's going out for little league or a spontaneous game of tag in the neighbor's yard, your child may shy away from participating. Since you know that once he gets over that initial fear he'll have a great time, it makes sense to help the process along.

Five-year-old Lilly had been asking to take tap-dancing lessons for two years, ever since she saw Gregory Hines hoof it up on "Sesame Street." But after her first class she announced she was never going back because she didn't like the other girls, most of whom knew one another. It wasn't that the girls were mean or even more experienced than Lilly; they were simply an unknown quantity. Her mother's offers to make introductions for her through their mothers elicited no response. But when she reminded Lilly of a similar experience—her first days at summer camp a few months earlier—Lilly perked up. "After only a few days you knew all their names and had started making friends. Let's figure out how to remember the names of these new girls, and after a few classes, they'll be like old friends, too," her mother promised. Then she suggested an "IT" technique for memorizing their names, a mind notebook Lilly could imagine writing them in. Buoyed by her own past social success, which she could *replay* in her mind, and the new Imagination Training game for learning the girls' names, Lilly walked confidently into her next ballet class.

Children often worry about their performance at social events. Will they be as funny as Tim? Will they do as well at playing games as Melissa? Parties are great occasions for a Takealong Friend who can sit in your child's pocket or on her shoulder to provide reassurance. This silent support can instill a feeling of instant confidence. With a Takealong Friend at her side, your child will soon start to think of herself as the kind of person able to overcome adversity. And quick relaxation techniques, such as deep breathing or playing a mind puzzle (see Chapter 11), can help calm the queasies when social jitters strike.

Taking the Strange out of Strangers

Even the most social youngster can be thrown by an unfamiliar adult, and sometimes for the most unlikely reasons. Emily, a very outgoing three-year-old, was terrified by a doorman at her grandparents' apartment building simply because he tried to amuse her by putting on a Donald Duck–like voice. It happened only once, but even months afterward Emily would ask fearfully, as she and her parents approached the building, "Is that man going to make that bad noise again?" And she did not want to enter the lobby. It didn't matter that the doorman never put on the duck voice again; that one time stuck with her. Emily needed to be desensitized to the fear. To accomplish this, her mother gave her a coping mechanism: to focus on her feet striking the pavement and then the tile floor of the lobby and also to hum, which would cover up any unwanted sounds. (Alternatives included the Finger Circle and holding Mommy's hand as they walked by the doorman.) She told Emily, "You know that doorman is really nice; in fact, he's a friend of Grandma and Grandpa's. But if you don't like him, then just look at your feet when we walk by, and you'll be safe." This particular approach actually accomplished two things at the same time: By explaining that the doorman was a friend, Emily's mother provided a reality check; and by offering an Imagination Training technique, she acknowledged the fear and helped Emily conquer it. The next step was to plant the idea: "I'll be here with you as long as you want, but someday when you get big, you may want to visit Grandma and Grandpa alone, and by then I'm sure it will be okay."

It takes surprisingly little to create a negative reaction. Children may pick up on an item of clothing, a facial feature, or some other physical characteristic, from a beard to imposing height or weight. If the person who causes anxiety is a relative, a close family friend, or an acquaintance who simply can't be avoided, such as the doorman, Imagination Training can come to the rescue. Have your child imagine that bearded Cousin Phil is one of Santa's brothers; very tall Cousin Harold might be compared to Aladdin's genie or a favorite real-life basketball player.

Relating to Relatives

Almost all of us have had an overbearing Aunt Tillie in our lives. You know, the relative who always pinched your cheek so hard it hurt and made you run the other way. Now it's your child's turn to face the pressure and anxiety. Chances are that his response is to shy away from dealing with her at all. And of course the more timid he appears, the more sweet Aunt Tillie presses for close contact! But no amount of toys and gifts from her or pleading from you can induce him to sit on her lap or give her a hug. There is an unhappy impasse for everyone concerned. Here's how to bridge the gap.

To initiate some movement from your child, start with a less painful prospect. Say, "It's okay not to sit on Aunt Tillie's lap, but you do have to come over and sit with me and talk with her." Since a child's apprehensions often fade over time, once some degree of familiarity has been established, you might end the visit by saying how nice it would be to hug Aunt Tillie good-bye and demonstrate it yourself first. If you continue to meet resistance, suggest this Imagination Training idea: "Look into Aunt Tillie's pretty blue eyes when you feel uncomfortable next to her, and you'll see in them how much she loves you." If your child is very agitated by the visit, give him a relaxation technique to help calm him, such as staring at a familiar picture on the living room wall or even his own fingernail. You can try to involve him in the solution to the awkward feeling her visit creates in him by saying, "I know you don't like to kiss her. That's okay. I don't like to kiss everybody either. But can you think of another way to let her know we care?" His answer will become the cornerstone of the solution.

The New Baby-sitter on the Block

Fear of baby-sitters presents a unique challenge. One solution to "sitter stress" centers on making the sitter, not you, the parent, the child's point of focus. After all, it is the sitter who has to win over your children; you do not have to convince them that the baby-sitter is truly okay. Prepare the sitter so that he or she can use Imagination Training techniques to conjure up images that portray him or her as fun, cheerful, and safe. She can be the embodiment of a Takealong Friend and create the corresponding environment, either real (using household items as props) or imagined. It might be helpful to find out from the children what they want the baby-sitter to be and let the sitter know in advance how to become that character.

The Neighborhood Bully

As kids get older, I am asked by concerned parents what to do about bullies. A lurking bully can make life unpleasant for just about everyone. Obviously the imagery of the Takealong Friend has its limitations. He or she cannot physically come to your child's aid and prevent a black eye and a bruised ego. Start by giving your child a better understanding of the problem. Explain that the bully is an insecure person who wants to show off to make himself feel better. It's even okay to feel sorry for the bully; he makes everyone feel miserable because inside he feels miserable himself. Concentrate on practical ways your child can diffuse the unpleasant situation, with

When Your Help Isn't Enough

How can you tell when outside help is needed? Use the three spheres of childhood activity to determine if you have a bona fide problem: school, home, and interaction with peers. If you notice that your child is experiencing problems or anxiety in any one of those areas, getting professional help is a decided elective. If problems show up in two areas, there is a spillover, and getting help is strongly suggested. Problems in all three areas means that help is virtually mandatory because now the child has nowhere to take refuge.

Look at the situation from an adult perspective. Suppose you and your spouse are quarreling and you're having a generally rotten week at home. You might take the opportunity to immerse yourself in work. Or let's say your boss is making life miserable for you at the office; a very common response is to turn to your spouse for support and sympathy. As a survival technique, you use one area as a refuge from the other. Problems arise when you feel there's nowhere left to turn. If you can't compensate for domestic infighting and you can't function well at the office either, it means that whatever you have been using as a compensatory method is no the goal of avoiding a fight. If possible, try to change your child's class or after-school activity schedule to avoid or at least minimize contact, and enlist the aid of other classmates (remember the adage about safety in numbers). It may be worth an attempt to talk out the situation with the bully. "Armed" with a Takealong Friend or a good-luck charm for moral support, your child might be able to make a friend of the bully; friends are often what bullies have in short supply. Help your child prepare for the encounter by having him imagine what he will say to the bully. This direct approach is often better than you or a teacher intervening.

Sometimes a fight is the inevitable outcome and your child may

longer working. When your coping mechanism breaks down, you are unable to keep your problems isolated and you need outside help. The same rules hold true for children.

Many of a child's social fears can be remedied by use of the Imagination Training techniques that are the core of this book. The most common social insecurities are discussed in this chapter. But other, deep-seated problems may require a more clinical evaluation. The first line of defense outside the home may be your pediatrician. Some doctors are very knowledgeable and open to discussing social problems. As part of a routine checkup, parents should ask their pediatrician about common behavioral problems such as the inability to get to sleep, trouble with eating, and so forth. Based on the kinds of responses you get, you should be able to form an opinion as to whether that doctor is behaviorally oriented. If you receive mechanical, textbook-type "solutions," your pediatrician is probably not a good source for effective answers. Other avenues of exploration can and should include friends with children, your clergyman, and school personnel. If these don't prove helpful, your pediatrician should be able to refer you to a specialist in child psychology.

not be able to just "walk away." While you would not encourage your child to begin a fight, if a fight is unavoidable, then you want him (or her) to do the very best that he possibly can, not just stand there and get punched. In this situation a little Imagination Training can go a long way toward boosting your child's self-confidence. Prepare your child for the possibility by explaining that "if a fight starts, you will see your own secret inner strength appear. It will make you fight better than you think you can and you'll notice that his punches won't hurt as much as you might think." This imagery is based in fact: In the excitement of a fight, the body produces adrenaline and endorphins that act as painkillers. If the discussion has already gotten this technical, give a "visual aid" by adding, "Once you get angry enough, these chemicals pop right into your blood." It is very helpful when you can take a normal body response that might seem frightening, such as a rapid heartbeat, and convert it into one that the child believes will make him stronger or better able to perform a task. Relaxation techniques and improved self-confidence have an added bonus. The more secure a child appears, the less likely he is to get picked on (bullies tend to go after kids they're sure they can intimidate). It sounds strange, and I'm not advocating fighting, but "survivors" report that the fighting can be less painful than a bruised ego or the *fear* of the fight.

These are some of the most common instances of social insecurity. Others crop up in school when children have to speak before the class or an audience (as discussed in Chapter 5), or later, in the preteen or teen years, when they start dating. Anxiety and apprehension can turn up nearly anyplace your child interacts with new people in new environments. The older a child gets and the more he or she is involved in varied activities, the more demand there will be for social skills. By using the tools of Imagination Training, you can help your child build a foundation of self-confidence that will see him or her through all the important social interactions of a young life.

School Daze

Getting Kids to Want to Go and Do Well

DO YOU REMEMBER THE first time your daydream during school hours was rudely interrupted by a teacher's command to step up to the blackboard? "Mr. Brown, would you please come here and diagram this sentence for the class?" Your heart races, the adrenaline flows, the mouth gets dry, and all your well-learned lessons dissipate as you walk to your doom as if it were your final stroll down death row. There are some kids who gleefully zip to it, of course, strutting with confidence and ready to capture and hold everyone's attention. But this is a small subgroup of children who like and seek the center of attention, the two or three kids who always have their hand up in class, waiting to be called on and wanting to be noticed.

Unfortunately, most parents discover that their children are more likely to shy away from the spotlight and seek anonymity. Have you ever seen junior high school students together at an event? They're all dressed the same, conforming to the prevailing style of the day. Pick out a crowd of them, and they all look like your child! They essentially go out of their way to wear the same uniform that prevents anyone from being singled out of the group. Any instance where one might be pushed to the forefront may cause an experience that can be both terrifying and traumatic.

School-related anxiety strikes long before the junior high years, and educators and child psychologists agree unanimously that schooltime fears are a primary issue that should be addressed as early as possible. School is, in essence, your child's workplace. He may spend up to one-third of each day in that environment, between regular classes and after-school activities. Performance at school and the ability to respond well in class and during tests have a lot to do with building one's self-esteem, as a child and later as an adult. When a child feels inadequate and can't perform to expectations, a poor self-image may develop. And it easily turns into a vicious cycle: Children with low self-esteem often do poorly in school and may suffer when their mistakes are ridiculed or amplified by schoolmates; in turn, their anxiety level grows and becomes evermore pervasive. Many schoolday apprehensions occur when children are caught in an embarrassing situation that makes them stand out, especially in front of their peers. (This fear ranks as high as the fear of being physically hurt.) But the crisis can start before your child takes even one step into the classroom. Just getting him out the front door can be tough. Here's how to get your child off on the right foot from the beginning.

Calming Preschool Panic

These days it is fashionable and often necessary to send children to preschool as early as age two. Bear in mind that preschoolers like predictability, a set pattern repeated day in and day out that lets them know what is expected. While the normal reaction to a child who fusses about going to preschool is to assume that he is too young or the school too overwhelming, his discomfort is more likely to come from the absence of a predictable, everyday pattern. A two- or three-day-a-week school means that your child doesn't know what to expect from one morning to the next. Frequently the child who resists that schedule will do fine going every day (and your only worry will be explaining why there's no school on the weekends!). Don't open the door to negotiation by asking if he wants to go more often; it's really your decision. As the saying goes, just do it.

One mistake parents often make with preschoolers is to talk too much or to "overexplain" each situation. "This is a great place, there are lots of toys, the teachers are nice, you'll meet new friends . . ." and on and on. You'll quickly have your child sensing your own anxiety and responding the same way. Though a two-year-old can't verbalize the thought "If Mom is so insecure, why should I be secure?" she can certainly act it out. The best approach is to drop off your child at the school using a loving but very matter-of-fact manner. Saying "I know you feel nervous, but everything will be okay" is more reassuring than having a long discussion. Despite your own very real anxiety about sending your little one off for the first time, the benefit of getting her there and acclimated is an important step in her socialization that will set a very positive example to draw on as she gets into the higher grades.

Children do need help getting acclimated, and there are ways to make the transition easier. Preschoolers are too young to use Imagination Training to allay any fears, but you can successfully utilize relaxation techniques such as counting numbers, saying the alphabet, or humming a favorite song while you're taking them to school. (Sometimes these simple techniques are excellent for older kids, too.) To cope with any initial discomfort after you leave them there, distractions work best. The teacher will have to initiate these, and skilled early childhood educators know how to get a young child's attention away from a mom who's trying to escape unnoticed. A tangible reminder of home in the form of a favorite toy or book or blanket will make the new surroundings homier—it's akin to the Takealong Friend for the older child who needs reassurance. If your child doesn't already have an established favorite, work together to create one or let him choose something different each day. Frequently these playthings get tucked into the child's cubby-hole along with his coat and don't get touched again until it's time to go home, but bringing one along acts as the bridge between the familiar and the new. Some preschools ask parents to bring in family photos, which are taped in the child's cubby; if there are any late-day separation anxieties, a quick look at the photo usually reassures the child that he has not been abandoned, and this seems to work as well as if the parent were actually there.

A final word on separation. While you are there, your child will stay focused on you. Your departure allows your child to focus on something else, to quickly become immersed in a number of varied activities. The parent who lingers is not acting in the child's best interest, just as a worried look on a parent's face when leaving says she is not confident the child is safe and sound.

Kindergarten Calamities

Before you know it, preschool days are over, and you're facing the next schooltime challenge, the school bus. For some youngsters the bus becomes an exciting adventure; for others it's a trip to oblivion. Keep in mind that what seems to be a fear of going to school may only be the fear of getting on the bus. Once again, the direct approach with a warm but nonnegotiable, positive presentation works best. But with a five-year-old you now have the opportunity to use Imagination Training to make the ride enjoyable. Help your child imagine the bus turning into her favorite mode of transportation—real (an airplane like the one that took the family on that great vacation to Florida) or imagined (Cinderella's pumpkin coach). Using the familiar makes her feel comfortable, but added imagery can also make the ride exciting. The driver becomes the pilot or coachman who will take her to a fun place for children and, after all the fun, will return her back home just as easily. She should "pack" for her trip by tucking something personal from home into her lunchbox or knapsack.

For some children the anxiety has to do with who is behind the wheel. Just think about it: Would you have wanted to take a ride on Ralph Kramden's bus? In the driver's defense, it's probably not easy to haul around dozens of screaming children, but your child interprets the driver's attitude in a very personal way. When he tells you that the bus driver isn't all that friendly, acknowledge his feelings, then try to have him focus on what bothers him the most. Ask "What does he do that makes you feel uncomfortable?" Once you pinpoint the problem—"He never smiles" or "He always yells at us"—ask "What do you think would happen if you tried to smile first when you got on the bus?" or "Suppose you said hello to him as you climb onboard. What do you think he'd say?" Help your child see the benefits of being the one to break the ice.

Kids who have not attended preschool find themselves in a double dilemma as they enter kindergarten. Getting used to separation via the school bus and dealing with perhaps the first nonhome environment ever encountered has many kids teary-eyed and confused. Thankfully, Imagination Training offers a variety of valuable tools. Your child has probably already established a few "good-luck" possessions that make him feel safe and go everywhere with him. The Takealong Friend can also be very reassuring, especially for the child who may now be hearing from his new classmates that carrying around a doll or teddy is "for babies."

While magic charms can be very effective, their loss may set off a panic reaction. And if they are not immediately replaceable, you're figuratively dead in the water! I've found that there is a special advantage to having a pair of shoes that empowers the child to do something he or she ordinarily wouldn't. Everybody who has seen *The Wizard of Oz* remembers the powers of protection that Dorothy's ruby slippers afforded. A similar mind-set can be created if you go out to purchase a pair of new shoes for school. Unlike special jewelry, for instance, which a very young child risks losing, even the most careless child rarely loses his shoes! Special socks, belts, and underwear (like superhero and superheroine T-shirts and underpants) are unlikely to get lost and are equally effective.

Facing the Class: It's Elementary

Up to this point we have been dealing with a school environment that is mostly play and socialization, with little or no emphasis on academics. As your child goes through the grades of elementary school, junior high, and high school, awaiting him is a whole new gamut of experiences that are sure to test his mettle and that could potentially unravel the security of childhood. Most of these education-related qualms have to do with performance at the blackboard and taking tests. Using esteem-building Imagination Training techniques early on can give children the solid base of "school security" needed to do well throughout their academic career.

Why do some kids go into a panic at the blackboard? The fact is that most people—including adults—don't like to have everybody focused on them. To your child, standing alone in front of a class allows all her classmates to scrutinize the way she looks, her clothing, her hairstyle, and every other detail. Even more important, they feel ominously vulnerable, open to criticism or even ridicule from an audience of unforgiving judges. Make one mistake on the blackboard, and soon the entire school (the virtual world to a child) knows about her folly. Just the anticipation of waiting to be called on can be nerve-racking. When we were learning to read in elementary school, the teacher would go up and down the rows of desks and have every student read a few paragraphs. We could see our turn coming at us like a tidal wave and felt anxious about picking up the narrative at just the right spot. The panic over not stumbling on any words made a few of my schoolmates turn pale as their time to perform became imminent.

Of course, preparation for school is important, but the personality of your child may be the deciding factor. There are many children who do their homework and are well prepared and yet panic when called on. These are the students who can best utilize Imagination Training strategies to develop confidence and a relaxed approach. The main goal of the strategies in this section is to teach your child to focus on the schoolwork when standing at the blackboard rather than be distracted by thoughts of having to give a "performance" before the class.

A simple idea that can easily be practiced at home is the "rule" for the right way to write on the blackboard. This forces your child to concentrate on the mechanical act of writing rather than on whether or not she'll be able to do it. Be very precise: "Hold the chalk between these two fingers and press very hard." This strategy creates a ritual that becomes the focal point and in turn offers the child a sense of security. Elaborate on it with this further suggestion: "If you press hard with the chalk, then your classmates can all see what you're writing, and they'll think you're smarter." Although the two thoughts don't seem to make any real sense together, when a parent makes a statement and follows through with a logical conclusion, a child is likely to believe it. And if a child believes he will perform better if he presses hard on the chalk, he usually will.

A similar confidence booster, and something just as easy to do as pressing hard on chalk, is suggesting that the child speak up when addressing the class. Offer this theory: "If you speak loudly, you will look as if you're smart. And if you look smart, the rest of the class will think of you that way." Expand the performance rituals to a short series of moves your child can remember and focus on: "When called on in class, stand up straight, look people in the eye, and speak with a strong voice. Then, even if you do make a mistake, people will still think that you're smart because you look like you are!" It may sound lengthy to your child, but it only takes a few seconds for him to actually do it.

The advantage of all these blackboard tricks is that they offer instant success, but the Finger Circle is particularly well suited to the fear of being called on in class. It's easy for your child to use the hand he isn't writing with and to keep it undetected in a pocket.

"Acing" the Test

Some parents may find that their offspring have no problem performing in the limelight, but their focus disintegrates when taking a written test. For the problem test taker, we can offer a somewhat different approach. The idea is to get these children to focus on the questions while excluding nearly everything else around them. Ironically, some of the things that can help young people do well may be contrary to their personalities. For instance, a disorganized or sloppy child often finds that studying and taking a test in very neat clothing makes him more focused because with the realization that his body is neat comes the ability to stay on track. Similarly, the child who is very uptight and keeps everything tidy and organized may do better if she relaxes her clothing or appearance and, in turn, her mind.

The best examples of relaxation/focusing imagery for problems of test performance are those that provide a hyper-focus on the test itself. If the child can achieve a high degree of focus, he may forget all the fears and apprehensions that accompanied him into the classroom. Some children respond to the concept of envisioning a bright light beaming down on the exam paper and highlighting it above anything else. Say, "Imagine that a bright light is coming over your shoulder. You can make it brighter by turning up a switch in your mind. And the brighter you can make it in your mind, the better you will be able to concentrate."

For a written test, pencil tricks replace the chalk tricks at the blackboard. Give your child a "special" box of pencils to be used just for test taking and have her go through the motion of sharpening each one right before the test begins; also make the suggestion that "sharp pencils mean a sharp mind." To increase her ability to hyper-focus, you might also suggest that she use a lucky pencil to under-line each question as she goes through the test or check off each question as she reads it. This technique has a calming action that improves self-confidence and is especially helpful for the child who is so flustered she doesn't take the time to read and comprehend the questions.

Lucky charms reserved just for test taking—from the magic penny to a special piece of jewelry or clothing, even a hair ribbon—will also help empower your child. The choices are limitless, although the best solutions for your child often evolve from your discussions and her imagination as you explore together what kind of imagery might sustain her attention. Another confidence booster is to have the child write a note to herself just before an exam begins that says "I am going to do very well on this exam." It may sound corny, but it combines the power of positive thinking with the elements of a good-luck charm.

Things That Go Bump in the Night and Other Frights

Help for Dream and Daytime Demons

WHETHER IT'S THE BOGEYMAN, a dark hall closet, or just the unseen presence of something lurking in the backyard bushes, the fears that kids have of the unknown are usually dependent on their ages. As your child outgrows one set of fears that suddenly seem rather silly, a new set arrives to take their place.

Beginning at some point between eighteen months and two years of age, children start to realize that things out in the world can hurt them. They start to be afraid of abstract things because they don't yet have the experience to know which specific things are dangerous. Mental creations like the bogeyman characterize abstract ideas that we find frightening. That's why when kids approach three years of age they suddenly become wary of dark closets, shadows, and other similar entities.

At about five years of age they realize that shadows are just shadows and that the hall closet is only filled with Dad's old junk. Now they become afraid of things that can violate their space—they have visions of fires in the house, robbers, and other terrors intruding on their safe haven. By the time they turn seven, their fears center on outside forces that can harm them: murderers and kidnappers and things that can cause pain or even death. Child abuse and abduction stories in today's headlines may make these possibilities seem real and make your child all the more fearful.

Many of these fears are justified, and some are even protective. It's really not so bad for youngsters to be afraid of a fire starting in the house or of being grabbed by a stranger as long as these ideas do not become overly consuming. In fact, many fears are part of our survival mechanism, deep-rooted as protection against the unknown.

The Bogeyman and Other Dream Demons

Children often incorporate being scared into their play, as do adults who might ride on a giant roller coaster. People like being brought to the brink of danger. This gives the feeling of being brave while simultaneously allowing one to be safe. Similarly, kids get a thrill from being told a scary story from the secure vantage of a parent's lap. Unfortunately, when it's time for the parent to say good night and leave the room, the same imagery may produce a nightmare as the child's sense of security is gone and there is no outside help to cope with the fright.

A perfect example of this dichotomy happened to four-year-old Alexandra who recently relocated with her parents from the city to a rural home with a forest bordering the backyard. Late one night her father heard what sounded like a large animal (probably a deer) crunching branches underfoot as it walked through the woods. The next day Alexandra heard her dad recount the story to her mom and was both thrilled and a little frightened as she imagined the possibilities of what the animal had been. She asked many questions about the incident and was reassured that it was certainly nothing that could bother the family or get in the house. Two nights later, however, she woke up from a nightmare linked to the story. Even so, the next day she insisted on having her father retell the story and demanded another recounting shortly before bed, a ritual that went on for weeks—along with a nightly nightmare! Each day the story, questions, and reassurances were always the same; each night her dreams turned the events into something alarming. But she still wanted the story retold for her and for each relative and friend who visited the new house. Eventually she even took over the role of storyteller although only her father had actually heard the noise. And despite the fact that she thrilled to the story when Dad was around, the nightmares continued unabated for a few more weeks until the whole issue died down.

Alexandra's fears about the unknown forest walker were soon replaced by general questions such as, "Can animals get into our house?" and even more specifically, "What would a bear do if it got into our house?" Hoping to avoid any further nightmares, Alexandra's father began using one of our core strategies, the alternate image to help fight off the fear. He began by saying, "Now, of course, you already know that there are no bears in this neighborhood. But even if there were, who is the toughest and strongest person you know who could scare away any bear that came around?" Of course the answer was "You, Dad!" Dad went on to illustrate the point further by embellishing on his natural ability as a bear fighter to put the issue to rest for good. This strategy can be used for dealing with monsters lurking in the basement or under the bed or outside the house.

I'd like to stress that kids, especially when they're very upset, tend to be more reassured by directive language than by long conversations. If you have a two-year-old who wakes up screaming about monsters in the closet, say, "There is no such thing as a monster. This looks scary but it really isn't. Anyway, we wouldn't let monsters into our house!" This comforts a child better than a long discussion that tries to explain away the monster: "I'll show you a book with a monster, but if there were really monsters, they'd all look the same in books, and there would probably be photographs instead of drawings . . ." and so on. This usually turns into the "never-ending story," and your reassurances get lost in the muddle.

An alternative to your being the hero is to let your child create his own image of a "dream hero." This character may even take the form of the child himself. Have him go to sleep dressed in his favorite superhero pajamas (or on his favorite superhero sheets or under the superhero comforter); this image may then transfer to a dream in which the child will feel empowered to defeat all comers.

There's a good reason that young children (and many adults!) have always gone to sleep hugging a stuffed animal or something familiar: The object empowers them with strength and a sense of not being alone. It makes an excellent relaxation tool, especially if you add the suggestion that Fuzzy will do his part to scare away any meanies that pop into your child's dreams. If your child has outgrown sleeping with a stuffed toy, empower an object like a magic penny that she can keep under her pillow, knowing that when endangered in a dream, the penny will protect her and ensure that no harm will come her way. Children are very creative and it makes sense to ask them what they would find reassuring. Let them build the path to follow, then you can enhance it.

Bugs and Other Daytime Creepy Crawlies

I am often asked to explain the fear of bugs. Some behaviorists cite this as a learned fear. However, I and many others believe this may actually be a deep-seated biologic fear based on the assumption that most people, especially children, can't distinguish which bugs are harmful and which are not. If one can't make that distinction, maybe it's better to be afraid of all of them. If you watch children, you'll notice that their fear is not simply associated with the size of the bug and it is disproportionate to the amount of harm it can do.

To cope with this kind of fear and those of animals, plants, fish, and reptiles (snakes and lizards), you can provide a dose of reality testing. Point out that "some bugs are scary, but some are cute. This one is okay, but this one isn't." This will change a generic fear into one that is more specific.

If you are in an environment where harmless bugs simply can't be avoided, guided imagery and/or distraction techniques will help. Try applying a lotion (bug repellant is best) as you suggest the imagery of a shield that will have a repellent effect: "I'm covering you with a special shield that can keep you safe." If you don't have any tangible aids at your disposal, create some logical reasoning that sounds as if it's based on fact. "If you wear yellow, mosquitoes will bother you [some insects are, in fact, attracted to certain colors], but if you are wearing green [or whatever color your child has on], they may stay away because they hate that color!" A magic penny, rock, or branch cut from a nearby plant can be empowered for further protection. One little girl I know lost her fear of bees because her father convinced her that the smell of her bubble gum was a bee repellent. (Of course, children with an allergy to beestings must be taught appropriate precautions.) Another parent convinced his daughter that "an old Indian trick to ward off flying insects is to carry a dandelion or other small flower in your pocket." Parents who might be worried about the effect that these little fibs will have on their relationships with their children may liken them to Santa, the Easter bunny, and the tooth fairy. There will be plenty of time to clear up any inconsistencies between childhood fantasy and reality later on. Of course, an excellent alternative would be to ask your child what she thinks will keep the bugs away and then offer encouragement: "That's a great idea! I bet it will work. Let's try it right now." And some parents feel more comfortable referring to fib-truths as "magic" colors or shields to differentiate them from real truths.

A child's fear of creepy crawlies can also be modified by the concept of "attachment." The idea is to give her one bug to focus her fear on to the exclusion of all others. By attaching your child's fear of all bugs to one specific bug and then telling her to avoid that particular one, you enable her to be comfortable around all the others. Explain it this way: "If you stay away from this bug, you'll be okay because this bug can really hurt you. All the other bugs in the yard are friendly and won't hurt you." To keep the distinction clear—to keep your message from getting lost—try to get your point across with as little discussion as possible.

Thunderstorms and Other Big Bangs

During frightening situations such as loud thunderstorms, you might try storytelling or using imagery to help your child feel more comfortable. "Do you remember last winter when we went sledding? The sled was a pretty red, and it had a long rope in front and was very secure. We were dressed to keep us nice and warm—you were wearing your blue coat and yellow hat. First I pulled you along a very pretty trail, then to the top of a very big hill. You told me that you were afraid, but you were very brave that day. First I went down the hill with you, but then you did it all by yourself. What a really fun day we had." This reminiscence has two advantages: It takes your child somewhere else during a scary situation, and it also reminds her of another time when she felt afraid and achieved a positive outcome after gaining control.

Medical Mayhem

Easing the Anxiety of Office Visits

WHY ARE MOST KIDS afraid of the doctor and the dentist? Parents logically surmise that it's the fear of pain; however, this fear also comes from the initial and greater fear of losing control. Imagination Training helps return some of that control to your child and makes these necessary examinations easier for both of you.

Overcoming Pediatrician Panic

A child's apprehension about visiting the doctor is a developmental change that manifests itself gradually as the child's awareness blossoms. Most infants up to one year really don't mind going to the doctor. Since they cannot anticipate medical procedures such as vaccinations, their protestations must lie elsewhere. They may cry because they don't like the crinkle of the examining table paper or having all their clothes off. Parents should keep an eye out for the specific things that bother their baby the most and simply try to avoid them. If it's the crinkly paper, bring a receiving blanket or towel that you can put over it. If your baby seems to object to the table itself, your pediatrician may be willing to perform the examination with the baby held on your lap. A receiving blanket is also handy to drape over the baby who doesn't like being naked.

Naturally, the viability of adopting various alternatives will depend on the personality of the pediatrician. Some are more rigid than others. Of vital importance is for both patient and parents to feel comfortable with this doctor. Remember that children see their pediatrician far more often than adults see an internist and you're going to be in this relationship for many years. When possible, parents should choose a practitioner they're compatible with. In my experience the best doctors are the ones who can shift gears and adapt to the personalities and situations involved. Some physicians play right into this role, while others do not have the patience or time. It's up to you to judge your and your child's reaction to a doctor before settling in.

Growing Pains

At some point between twelve and fifteen months of age, babies who have been perfectly cooperative suddenly begin to develop negative tendencies: No matter what you offer him, the baby rejects it. And this behavior isn't limited to the doctor's office; it becomes his everyday approach to life. Expect your baby to reject diapering, bathing, dressing—all the simple acts that you performed previously without incident. Recognize it as a stage of normal development and be prepared to use a bag of distraction tricks for those second-year office visits. This behavior generally begins to disappear after age two and a half; the same child who yelled his way through an entire exam now becomes cheerful and cooperative, and may even sit on the doctor's lap!

Aside from these developmental changes that may govern a child's receptiveness toward medical treatment, the procedures invoking the most ballyhoo for child and parent are those involving a needle—an injection or blood test. Most infants of less than fifteen months seem to do better when the task is accomplished quickly and with little fanfare. An injection is over so fast that no diversions are necessary, although a few can be distracted before or after the shot by using a bright light or a brightly colored object. Parents may opt to use nonverbal calming techniques such as rocking, stroking, or hugging and asking for the injection to be given while the baby is comfortable and secure on Mom's lap.

On Pins and Needles

Some behaviorists believe that the fear of needles is a basic instinct. It is certainly one we carry through life: During my tenure as an infantry battalion surgeon during the Vietnam conflict, it always amused me that combat-hardened Rambo types, immune to the sights and sounds of war, couldn't handle a simple tetanus shot any better than the average preschooler: "Are you sure I really need that shot, Doc? Looks like an awfully big needle!"

I've noticed that many children don't come to the office dreading the possibility of a shot—they may not even know what one is unless they've heard about it from a peer or witnessed a baby sister or brother's early inoculations—but they do become afraid the instant they sense the preparation. Sometimes the smell of rubbing alcohol and the sight of the syringe elicit that fear. But whether your child is naively unaware or bordering on hysteria, there are a number of techniques and accompanying diversions appropriate for each instance. Review the four different approaches to needlephobia discussed in the first half of Chapter 3.

One solution not addressed in that section is designed for the child who is really out of control, who needs you and two nurses just to hold him in the examining room. Unfortunately, having a rational discussion with a child who is irrational simply doesn't work. To handle only these very *extreme reactions*, exaggerating the pain and the consequences of noncompliance has proved to be an almost foolproof (albeit seemingly appalling) method. In your most serious but nonthreatening tone, say to your child, "You're getting this shot whether you like it or not. You have no control over that. But you *can* control whether or not it's going to hurt. If you move even the slightest amount, this shot will burn very, very much. But if you stay very, very still, you will hardly feel it." It's hard to believe the child's reaction afterward. Some are almost angry that it didn't hurt: "That's it? That was nothing!"

Let's break down the components of your startling declaration. You stated up front and unequivocally what was not in the child's control, yet at the same time you offered her control over one aspect of the situation—the degree of discomfort. Exaggerating the pain usually causes a child to remain focused until after the shot is administered. To some observers this use of psychological force may seem cruel, but in practice it is far kinder than the more common approach: hysterical negotiations that never seem to work. (You know that routine: You beg and plead while he screams and squirms.)

When it is necessary for blood to be drawn from the arm, a procedure that will take somewhat longer to perform than a simple shot, in my office we sometimes incorporate the tourniquet trick. I apply the tourniquet with the following practiced narrative: "I'm putting this bracelet on your arm so that you will hardly feel what I'm going to do. I want you to tell me when your hand or arm starts to feel tingly or achy." When the child gives me the go-ahead, I say, "That's great because now it's working, and you will hardly feel anything. You can even watch when I put in the needle."

In this technique I've empowered the tourniquet (you may even describe it as "the kind of armband the Indian medicine men wore" or one of Wonder Woman's cuffs) to do something (which definitely happens), enhanced with a little reasoning that isn't quite accurate but is certainly plausible. Telling children that the armband will make their arm "numb" or "sleepy" (depending on their age) and that they will hardly feel the needle sounds plausible even to the most savvy six-year-old. And believe it or not, because most kids really want to believe that their arm will go sleepy, most do! Younger children, usually four to six, prefer it if you refer to pain as "the hurt," "the ouch," or even "the owie." These words seem to make the thought of any discomfort easier for them to deal with.

Some blood testing can be done simply, but there are children for whom this will be their worst nightmare. (Always remember that these reactions have a lot to do with individual personality, and you should resist ridiculing such feelings.) It is also true that on certain days, at certain locations, and depending on who's doing the procedure, it will hurt less or more. But for some children, no matter what the setting or preparation, fear sets in, and little tricks can be helpful.

If more than a few drops of blood from the finger prick must be collected, you'll want to create a diversion that not only calms your child emotionally but also helps her to keep still. For the youngest child, humming, singing, or even soft talking is helpful because he will be drawn to Mom or Dad's familiar, reassuring voice. If you have a hand free (in some offices or clinics and depending on your child's age, you may be asked to hold her on your lap), singing and playing Where Is Thumbkin? with your fingers should provide enough distraction for the entire procedure, especially if you go through the "pointer," "tall man," and "ring man" choruses! With two free hands, showing pop-up books and those with pull tabs that flip the picture on a page work nicely. By age five, most children are willing to do imagination play with you. You begin the story as soon as the antiseptic used to cleanse the finger appears: "Let's make believe that we are going to take a walk through Mr. McGregor's garden. I see Peter Rabbit, his fur soft and shiny, hiding in the round, green, and purple cabbages. His fluffy cousin is sitting next to him. They've nibbled on some cabbage leaves, but they're still hungry. What vegetable should they eat next?" If your child isn't willing to participate but is helped by listening to you, continue the story on your own, describing each of the vegetables with as much sensory imagery as you can think of. The more detail you provide, the easier it is for your child to "see" the fantasy. So it's not just "carrots" but "long, bright orange carrots that crunch like cornflakes when Peter nibbles at them." Be sure to pick the adventure your child will enjoy most; it's almost impossible to fail if you retell the tale of her current favorite movie or book, or transport her to her favorite day-trip destination or a place she dreams of going.

Keep in mind that the needle prick or injection that didn't faze your child at all in the doctor's office can turn into a major ouch hours later. Rather than respond with "How can that possibly hurt you now?" use a tried-and-true "analgesic" such as kissing the boo-boo or offering a stuffed animal to squeeze to make the hurt go away. There can be some very real soreness following an injection or after blood was drawn. Before leaving the office, you might ask your pediatrician about applying an ice cube to the site or giving acetaminophen to relieve any discomfort should the need arise.

Keep Mum, Mom and Dad

Now I'd like to touch briefly on what not to do. Some parents assume that a lengthy talk of "preparation" before an office visit is beneficial. However, the more nervous the parent is about something, the more talking he or she feels it necessary to do. And sometimes the more talking the parent does, the more nervous the child becomes. I have found that especially for young children, talks of very short duration and with a minimal amount of explanation work best. I've seen parents begin preparing a child nearly two weeks in advance of a visit. By the time Junior goes in, he is absolutely off the wall!

It would be wrong to tell a three-year-old you're all going to visit Grandma and then show up at the doctor's office. On the other hand, you don't have to have an extensive discussion on the topic. A sound preparation for his third-birthday checkup might go something like this: "We're going to visit the doctor to see how nice and tall you've gotten." The younger the child, the shorter the prep time, and the nearer to the actual visit your talk should be. For a regular doctor visit, telling the child on the same day is fine.

Defusing Dental Hysteria

Colleagues of mine who are dentists tell me that there is an intrinsic fear of dentistry that parallels that of needles. Maybe it harks back to some caveman's first toothache and the extraction performed by a fellow cave dweller. Part of the trauma, as true for adults as for children, is that you can't talk while someone has his or her hands in your mouth and you are at the disadvantage of lying back in a vulnerable position, mouth wide open, unable to see anything the dentist is doing. Factor in the discomfort of the dentist's tools poking around inside his mouth, and it's no wonder kids shy away from dental appointments.

Your choice of dentist is of paramount importance. At the top of the criteria list is a dentist who sees children all the time. Word of mouth from other parents as well as recommendations from your pediatrician should give you a few names to investigate. A dentist needn't specialize in caring for children, but the best question to ask if you are considering a family dentist is whether he or she actually likes to have children as patients. Some family dentists may be phasing out their practices; the amount of effort needed to take on a small child is significant, and they may not have the patience to spend the amount of time needed. Others may not be interested in cultivating that market at all. Anything less than an enthusiastic response is a signal that you should look further. By the way, a quick scan of the office waiting room is very telling: If there are no children's magazines, books, or games in sight, this may not be the right practitioner for your child.

The personality of the dentist counts, too. Some dentists prefer no interference, or they may permit you to distract your child, inadvertently throwing the dentist off stride. A more flexible practitioner who has experience with children or who specializes in pediatric dentistry will have his or her own distraction techniques built into the procedures and may suggest you hold yours in reserve as backup. Some dentists rely on their own chatter to distract children; others provide visual targets to stare at or headsets that allow patients to listen to music or stories. Another approach is to "involve" the child by letting her touch a duplicate of each instrument or hold a mirror to watch (and help demystify) the exam.

If you as the parent must provide added distraction during a dental procedure, you must be careful to choose and implement techniques that won't become equally distracting to the dentist. To be truly effective you really need to clue the dentist into your ideas before you attempt them. When your help is needed, successful approaches involve techniques that draw on as many of the senses as possible—in this case, distraction with things that can be seen or heard. For example, you might stand in the child's sight line holding an object that your child can focus on. Like the effect of staring at a stage hypnotist's swinging pocket watch, staring at a "visual aid" will relax even the most tense child. Items with motion, such as a pinwheel, or with light, such as a little flashlight or even a Gameboy, work well and can be practiced beforehand. Audio distractions may take many forms, from the simple recitation of a favorite story (if the dentist permits) to listening to a Walkman with favorite music or a prerecorded story. Pop-up books are great for small children (remember that many dentists recommend a first visit before the age of two). Of course, your child's personality really determines the best "IT" tool. For instance, some children simply don't have the patience to become immersed in a story; they might be happier simply watching a pinwheel spin.

Once your child is old enough to engage in Imagination Training on her own, she can "escape" from her real surroundings and, in her mind, take the Cloud Copter to the Pillow Palace or any destination of her dreams. Kids with less imaginative powers can nonetheless empower themselves with the Finger Circle, cut off the pain with the Pinkie Pain Switch, or invoke their Takealong Friend to dull the discomfort, as we discussed in Chapter 3.

For the child who suffers a traumatic dental injury—an accident that knocks out teeth, for instance—there are other factors to deal with. The primary upset is due to pain, but certainly no less horrifying to the young patient is the flow of blood that can come from the gums and mouth. If you can keep calm, you can quickly reassure your child, turning the negative into a positive by saying, "I can see from the color of your blood that everything is okay. Good thing we saw that!" Many parents are equally stricken by the first sight of their child's blood. Calm yourself with the knowledge that it usually looks worse than it is, and then calm your child. Remember that almost any negative can be turned into a positive if you can create the right imagery.

After resolving the blood issue, quickly move on to dealing with the pain. If the child is quite upset, jump to any of the tried-and-true pain strategies, depending on the child's age: a new "toy"—any thought or object has the power to get her attention—an instant lucky charm, or one of the core concepts, such as the Pinkie Pain Switch. Just as it's important to know what physical steps you should take in an emergency, it makes sense to know in advance what calming techniques are most likely to work.

Who's the Boss: Taking Medicine and Beyond

How To Regain Control of Difficult Situations

A PATIENT'S MOTHER ONCE called me with what she considered a very perplexing problem and one she was at her wit's end to solve. Her three-year-old son Vincent periodically experienced irregular bowel movements, often culminating in excruciating constipation. Including "helpful" foods in his diet, such as raisins, prunes, and whole wheat bread, often helped, and Vincent knew that eating them made him "go" more easily. If a few days or a week passed without his having any of these foods, constipation was inevitable; and sometimes even the high-fiber approach wasn't enough. Once a month or so, the child would end up sitting on the toilet for up to an hour and crying, sometimes screaming, until nature took its course: "Mommy, I need some raisins right now!" After making certain there were no medical problems, I suggested a number of over-the-counter remedies, all of which involved taking a pill or drinking a liquid—simple, effective solutions to this common problem. Unfortunately, the child refused to accept the idea of taking anything, especially when under duress.

After a more intensive investigation of the mother's medicine-administering approach, I discovered that most of her attempts resulted in a protracted bargaining session under extremely unpleasant conditions and usually to no avail. So although help was at hand, the child would suffer, and the mother would back off and allow him to dictate how the situation would resolve itself. The phone call proved to be a good opportunity to tell Vincent's mom not only a few Imagination Training techniques that could be of use but also, and probably more important, to explain how to gain control over the problem he was experiencing. While this chapter discusses the often harrowing experience of getting your child to take medicine, it has a somewhat larger scope that addresses a particularly difficult part of parenting: how to handle the nonnegotiable aspects of life when kids protest against something they simply have to do, such as, going to school, following your rules, or swallowing a teaspoon of a medicine that doesn't come in cherry or grape.

Don't Be Afraid of Being a "Meanie"

Parents are often guilty of being overly dedicated to empowering their children and of treading too lightly when they act up for fear of insulting them. One of the most common errors noticed by pediatricians and psychologists is that of parents who talk to their children, even two- and three-year-olds, as if they were their peers. Some parents often look at giving a directive without an explanation as a sign of disrespect. Explanations should be given during daily discussions but not when you are giving a disciplinary message. Parents typically incorporate explanations with requests, such as, "Please do this because . . ." when "Please do this" would be enough. Young children often get upset with this speech pattern because it is confusing to them. Most three-year-olds are very rigid and concrete, seeking order in their lives. They don't want their peas to touch the carrots, or be given milk in their juice cup, or find the stuffed rabbit in their teddy bear's place on the bed. Explanations may be interpreted by

Setting the Ground Rules

The act of administering medication is a battleground where the wills of parent and child can clash head-on. The first key to success is to set the ground rules immediately. Without appearing mean or angry, you should firmly establish that there are some things in life the child can control and other things he or she simply can't. Make it crystal clear that this circumstance falls into the latter group and that he will take the medicine one way or another. That fact is non-negotiable, and you should state it as such right up front and in just that way. Leave no opportunity for options or negotiations.

There is room, however, to put Imagination Training into play. Remember that anxiety always makes an illness feel worse, and when a child is ill, dealing with pain or discomfort plus the prospect of being forced to take some dreaded form of medication will make

your child as meaning that it is not okay this time but may be okay next time—a condition that does not make him feel secure.

Most very young children want and need things to be very explicit with black-and-white, "this is good and that is bad" scenarios. They respond best to directives, not explanations. Explaining "why" often ends up creating a situation that requires negotiation for something that you had already deemed nonnegotiable, while giving a needless explanation, one often forgets to send the message of what specifically you want done. For example, instead of just saying, "Don't fight!"—a common decree in many households—parents say, "Don't fight because it isn't nice. Other children will get upset and won't want to come over, and someone might get hurt. And you remember how you didn't like the way it felt when you fell off the bed the last time." What happens is that the next time your child wants twenty minutes of your time, he'll hit the neighbor's kid, and then settle in for the next lecture. Parents often respond to a repeat of the misbehavior with "What's the matter with you? Didn't we just discuss this?" First, you must realize that "we" didn't discuss this; only you did!

his anxiety peak. But if presented correctly, any medication can have a very strong placebo effect, especially in younger children who are susceptible to the power of suggestion. In short, if a child believes the medicine will work, it probably will and it is more likely to work fast! By having your child take medicine right away, as soon as symptoms appear, you create the suggestion that the child is getting better by the moment.

Giving children medicine should be done with great bravado that can even make it sound like fun. "I'm giving you medicine, and it's going to make you feel better" offers a positive suggestion and increases your chances of quick and successful compliance. The less forceful "Now it's time to take your medicine," a neutral or even negative suggestion, is much less likely to receive a satisfactory response. When your child is defiant, reinforce your opening declaration with a strong follow-up, such as "The doctor said it's going to work fast," which adds the weight of outside authority. Empower

Second, you neglected to give the child a straight directive saying exactly what kind of behavior you expected. Third, you freely gave your child your time for doing the wrong thing. A fuller explanation might be appropriate if given at a time separate from the time of discipline. When the subject is taking medicine, "You have to take your medicine. It's going to make you better!" should be the extent of your message. You should avoid a running monologue: "If you don't take your medicine, you'll get sicker and have to go to the hospital, and then you'll miss school and your friends and . . ." You can see that the lengthier the reasoning, the more hidden and ultimately lost the real message becomes. A protracted explanation actually makes the true meaning of your words more difficult to comprehend. And remember, when directing young children to do things that are not negotiable, don't negotiate. I had a sign over my first child's bed that read "A person is a person no matter how small." Before bringing my second child home from the hospital, I took down the sign.

the child as an active participant by announcing that "the medicine will work even better and faster if you don't move/if you swallow it all/if you hold it in." Finally, you may add, "If you do what I'm telling you, this is all going to be over a lot faster than it takes to argue about it." Though your child can't control whether he'll take the medicine, he does get to decide whether or not the experience is to be pleasant. These days, most medicines have a tasty flavor, and unpleasantness is more likely to come from attitude than from the medicine itself.

When Actions Must Take the Place of Words

Distraction may be effective when giving young children medicine. When the child is engrossed in a video, a TV show, or a story, he will sometimes open his mouth for the spoon without giving it a second thought. This strategy works when you are dealing with a child who regards your directives as reasonable. However, in my practice I have encountered occasional children who absolutely refuse to swallow medicine and who require somewhat more strict methods for compliance. For this small group, while the child is held firmly in the parent's lap, the parent should proceed with the demeanor of a robot (not angry and not annoyed) and say, "If you spit this out, I'm going to give it to you again." Maintaining control in a robotic fashion tells kids that sooner or later they will have to give in. Even if it takes two hours the first time, your persistent approach sets the stage of experience, and the next time is bound to be more successful. At most, the process will have to be repeated two or three more times. But waver and negotiate, and a child will continue to challenge you as long as he feels that he has any possible degree of control. Part of the "game" here is that as he watches you freak out and get frustrated, it actually eggs him on! After your child takes the "hint" and swallows the medicine, it's time to bestow lavish positive reinforcement: "I'm really proud of you.

You're really growing up! What a good medicine-taker you are!"

With a little practice and a little imagination on your part to broaden the scope of this strategy, it won't be long before medicine-taking and other similar problems become rather routine.

A Spoonful of Imagery
Makes the Medicine Go Down

When it comes to easing the mechanics of taking medicine, Imagination Training can have a great benefit, especially for the child who is willing but simply doesn't know how to swallow a pill. For little children who have not yet learned and practiced the technique of swallowing it with a little water, taking one of those large-size antibiotics can be quite a daunting task. Yes, there are bubble gum–flavored liquids these days that some kids actually like, even similarly flavored chewables, but sooner or later every child is bound to struggle with sending a pill down a throat that seems much too small.

Start by having your child imagine that the pill is a favorite small food. Then you can have him pretend that his throat can change size to gobble up that food. You might suggest: "Your throat is a tunnel that you can make larger and larger. It's small at first, just about as wide as your thumb. Can you see it? Now when you press on your belly button, it gets wider and wider. Wow, I can see that it's really opening up and getting ready. Are you pressing that button because I can see that it's getting even wider now. That little pill won't have any trouble sliding right down!" Of course you should tell small children not to use this for any other purpose, that it's a trick for swallowing medicine.

Easing Aches and Pains

How To Make the Ouch Feel Better

EVEN AFTER TREATING HUNDREDS of children in my practice, I'm still amazed at how some kids seem to bounce back immediately from a fall-related scrape while others act as if they had lost a limb. Whether it's a minor accident, major trauma, or serious illness, your child's recovery time and amount of discomfort lie very much within his or her individual personality. With your help, Imagination Training can make the pain self-limiting and much more bearable.

It's rather difficult to determine how much of the pain is real and how much has been magnified. Pain has two distinct components: One is physical, and the other is the way it is perceived. Doctors know how to control the physical component of pain with pain relievers, anesthetics, ice, and other remedies, but parents can strongly affect the psychological component for their child. "Selective attention" (basically, ignoring the pain while focusing on something else) is often used by adults without their even realizing it. For example, a nagging headache develops while you're at work on an important project. You think to yourself, I don't have time for this headache, and you keep on working, focusing on the task at hand. When you're finished two hours later, you realize that your headache has not gone away. The physical component of the pain didn't change, but your perception of it did: By focusing on the work, you avoided thinking about the pain and were able to function normally. Professional athletes—such as the football player who plays with a separated shoulder or broken ankle—have raised these techniques to an art form.

Everyday Bumps and Bruises

With cuts and scrapes, if the parent takes charge by performing the "caregiving" process right away (cleaning the area and applying an antibiotic ointment and bandage), the care itself can become the point of focus rather than the pain. Saying "Let's make it stop hurting" plants the suggestion that the experience is limited. "When I clean off this scrape, it will hurt a lot less" creates an encouraging sequence of events. Talk about the experience and the process: "Look at the good color of your blood. It means that it's going to heal fast." Next, compliment your child and give her a sense of control. You promote her ability to help herself when you say, "I'm very proud of you for being so brave. When I put on this dressing, it will make it stop hurting."

If you have a hysterical child who is screaming uncontrollably, however, such rational conversation will be lost in the din. Avoid saying "It's not so bad," "Don't be a baby," and the hard-to-resist "Why weren't you more careful?" Instead gain your child's attention first by using calming mechanisms or distractions appropriate for his or her age, until you help him regain his control and composure. Rocking and stroking are best for younger children. Singing and humming work, too. Also, the child can focus on your voice while you explain what's happening. For older kids, suggest that you both try taking some deep breaths. You might even add, "Did you know that crying makes a boo-boo hurt more? But the more air you can fill your body with, the faster the hurt will go away." Try distraction for children of all ages. Bringing your child to watch TV, reading him a book, telling a story, and having him squeeze your hand are all excellent distraction techniques. Other things parents have been doing successfully for years are kissing the boo-boo or blowing on it to make it cool and feel better.

Techniques literally at your (or your child's) fingertips are having her count your fingers or blow on them as if they were birthday candles. Or have your child squeeze her fist (or even just a thumb) as tightly as possible. Say, "Imagine that all your pain is squeezed into your fist. Now open your hand and throw all the pain out of your body and into the air." An alternative is having her squeeze Mommy or Daddy's hand as you tell her you'll get rid of the pain for her.

Sometimes it's not the actual pain or even the sight of blood that's the problem but rather the surprise of the accident and the loss of control a child feels. Some children believe that the object that precipitated the injury violated them, and they become insulted. And an assault by an inanimate object can be embarrassing to children and adults alike. (Who hasn't at least once kicked an open drawer or chair that got in our way and "tripped" us?) One parent informed me that whenever her child had a mishap with an object, she actually encouraged him to vent his frustration with a short tirade against the offender. Shouting "Oh, that stupid chair!" works as a distraction from the pain as well as an adequate way for the child to save face by transferring the "blame."

The Serious Side of Pain

Once a child's illness has been thoroughly evaluated medically, Imagination Training may be useful when added to the treatment regimen. Those children who live with a chronic illness often have to face pain and discomfort every single day. And along with most chronic illnesses comes an emotional component that can and frequently does exaggerate the symptoms. For example, children with severe eczema tend to perspire when they feel nervous, and when they perspire, they tend to itch more. Then they scratch the afflicted area, itch more, and get more nervous about the condition as the cycle perpetuates itself.

Kids with a spastic colon usually have an overactive bowel that can lead to cramps or abnormal bowel movements. Although stress is not the cause, these children are more likely to experience cramps during stressful periods. And, of course, the more discomfort they experience, the more stressed they become. Stress causes pain, and pain causes stress, so breaking this vicious cycle is important. During cramping episodes it's helpful to have your child use Imagination Training to ease his discomfort. Suggest that he imagine an ocean with many waves that he can then gradually calm in his mind, making it go from very rough, wavy water to flat, shiny, smooth water. Tell him that the ocean is like his bowel: If he can imagine it getting smooth in the same way that he calmed the ocean, he can help make the cramps go away.

In many cases, matching the symptom your child is experiencing with a similar image, then having her think of an opposite thought, is a good pain-reducing technique. In the case of a headache, for instance, your child can imagine hearing a very loud noise or music, then concentrate on making it softer and softer.

For kids with asthma, wheezing is truly multifactorial; that is, the airway can close down because of irritants (such as cigarette smoke), allergens (such as pollen), infections (such as a cold), or even exercise. But anxiety can also kick it off, and any combination of these factors can precipitate an attack. When the child begins to wheeze, it makes him nervous, and he may wheeze even more.

For these and other common complaints, Imagination Training can help to break the stress-symptom cycle and make it easier for the child to cope with not only the demands of the illness but also the demands of its treatment. For the child with diabetes, for example, it may be the daily insulin shot rather than the diabetes itself that causes anguish. Stress seems to play a greater role as children become more social, when they realize they are different from other children, and they worry about fitting in, about looking or acting in a way that makes them stand out. Once they are old enough to experience such social "insecurity," they are old enough to learn what is going on inside them physiologically. Imagination Training can help them understand their body and become more comfortable inside it.

Asthma can be explained this way: "When your air pipes (or bronchial tubes) close up, they make a whistling sound. An asthma attack can be helped if you can make these air pipes bigger." A young asthma patient named Robert found relief by first focusing his attention on a spot on the wall, an object in the room, or even on his thumbnail, and then thinking about a place he loved to go, the beach he and his family often went to on vacation. As Robert imagined that beach, he relaxed more and more. Once he had "transported" himself to these happier surroundings, he imagined that his airway was a little straw with no air coming through it. Next he imagined that with every breath he took he could make the straw larger until it became the size of a giant tunnel. It helped him to hold two fingers together with a little space between them and then to open them as he made the tunnel larger. The tunnel became so big that Robert himself could enter and run through it.

Whenever he had trouble breathing, Robert found that by slowing his breathing he had the power to make his airway become larger and larger, just as he made the straw expand into a tunnel. It was quick and easy to do, but even more important, Robert believed that it worked. Through the power of his own imagination, he felt he had gained control over his illness.

Now, rather than panic whenever he got a wheezing attack at school or at the playground where he had no immediate access to his medicine, all he had to do was relax for a minute and focus on the imagery to open his airway. And even if medication was available, this was a good way to pass the time while waiting for it to work. Because he believed in "IT," Robert was eager to use it and used it quite effectively. Robert's outlook on life changed dramatically: Rather than fear many activities because they might bring on an attack, he started to approach new challenges with the eagerness that every little boy should have.

Elyssa uses Imagination Training for her severe eczema. She had often scratched her irritated skin so vigorously that she bled, and she was consumed by her ailment. With her mother's help she learned the mechanics of relaxing by focusing her attention on a single object—either a cloud in the sky, a piece of clothing, or a favorite toy—which helped to tune out her surroundings (usually she would pick the same object). Then she was able to take herself to her favorite place, which she called Grandma's "magic garden." There she would imagine that her itchy spot was surrounded by a cool breeze. As Elyssa relaxed, her mother talked a lot about making her skin feel better: "Feel the cool breeze cover your arm and take all the itchiness away. The coolness can make your skin tingle, it can make it numb and sleepy." The longer she felt the breeze, the more comfortable she became. In a short time Elyssa noticed that the itching was gone. She learned that she could use this imagery to stop itching wherever she was and without anybody else even knowing about it.

Once transported in their minds to a happier place, children may respond to putting on the Magic Glove that can numb their pain (as discussed in Chapter 3) or to the use of opposite imagery—thinking of their skin as being as rough as sandpaper and then imagining making it smooth.

Escaping to a favorite happy place is something every child can do in times of distress—whether the distress is prompted by a chronic condition like asthma or a more serious illness. To find out where your child's favorite place is, all you have to do is ask: "If you could go anywhere you wanted to go, where would you pick?" This assures that the child will focus on the image that has the most significance at this time.

When kids have a recurrent problem, practicing Imagination Training during times they are well can be very helpful. In that way they don't have to learn it when they're in distress, and they will be comfortable with the technique when they really need it. It is also useful to tell your child that he can use the same technique whenever he feels frightened or upset about something else.

You might want to review the Imagination Training techniques, the Magic Glove and the Pinkie Pain Switch, in Chapter 3.

Opposites Distract

Help your child match his or her symptoms to an image. By imagining that image becoming its opposite, he or she can help make the discomfort disappear. Practice the following contrasts:

Loud to quiet (noise)
Hot to cold (breeze, water)
Black to white
Wavy to flat (ocean)
Windy to calm
Big to little
Bright to dark (glowing circle on the wall)
Thin to wide (straw, tube, tunnel)
Rough to smooth (fabric or sandpaper)
Heavy to light (from lead to a feather)
Rainy to sunny
Wet to dry

Calms Without Qualms

Solutions for Special Problems

THROUGHOUT THIS BOOK WE have explored the causes for and solutions to the most prevalent social and physical fears that children face. In this chapter the focus is on a group of specialized situations that may occur over the course of your child's life. Although each one is challenging in a different way, you'll see that the same core concepts for coping with anxiety consistently come to the rescue.

I'd like to preface these stories by saying that you can't protect a child from every negative experience. If and when they do occur, it's important to maintain your perspective. On the one hand, never minimize your child's fears; you may find your son's recoiling from Santa absurd, but to him the feelings are real and need to be recognized. Don't make your child the subject of ridicule or punishment. Some of the most distressing emotional battles begin with overbearing parents ceaselessly pushing their kids to confront their anxieties head on and without parental help or understanding. Resist making an issue over something that is not a priority in your lives; when your child's fears collide with your expectations, it won't help if needless anger and disappointment set an emotional typhoon in motion. Identify the "big" issues, and don't make life's experiences a protracted battle or an endless test of wills. If you set out to do something that's supposed to be enjoyable for your child and he doesn't see it your way, have the flexibility to shift gears or try Imagination Training to turn the situation around in a nonconfrontational way. Remember that for your child the cornerstone of resolving anxiety is the security that comes from knowing that you're there to help.

Subduing Scary Santa

Elaine couldn't wait to get her son Kim to the mall for the two-year-old's first meeting with Santa; she had already picked out the spot on the mantel for the enlargement of the photo she had planned to have taken! Much to Elaine's chagrin, Kim found Santa downright frightening and refused to stand next to him, much less jump onto his lap. How could that be? We think of him, with his round, cheery face and warmhearted "Ho, ho, ho!" as a nurturing, pleasant, grandfatherly type. But just imagine what a young child's perception might be the first time he lays eyes on old Saint Nick: an oddly dressed stranger whose face is suspiciously obscured by a voluminous beard—overwhelming, threatening, and maybe even terrifying. Plus he's expected to sit in the guy's lap! Of course, your child's appraisal of Santa can and probably will change from year to year until he makes the same positive and immediate association we do. But being only two, Kim wasn't able to verbalize what specifically upset him about Santa. Preschoolers in particular often exhibit anxieties toward people based on their clothes or unusual appearance. The child is often not focusing on the whole person but on only one outstanding characteristic. You might be thinking that he's scared of Santa when it's simply Santa's beard. Keep in mind that kids are also more likely to view things in a polarized fashion—as totally great or totally awful—because they don't have a wealth of experience to fall back on. Elaine understood this when it was explained to her, but she still wanted to help Kim overcome his fear right away.

First, she was cautioned not to force the issue. From Kim's point of view there was no real urgency to resolve the problem; certainly a photo opportunity with Santa is not as important as adjusting to, say, sleeping in a first bed. However, there was a technique to desensitize Kim to the fear before the new year. Elaine started with a reality check, saying to Kim, "Sometimes Santas look scary, but the one we are going to see isn't." With Kim's uncle acting as a Santa stand-in without the beard and red suit, and providing the ho, ho, ho's, Elaine and Kim went through a few rehearsals, practicing what it would be like to see Santa at the mall; this role-playing is a form of Imagination Training with the focus on a nonthreatening Santa. She walked Kim through the steps of saying hello, sitting on Santa's lap, even smiling for the photo, and with a little practice, he began to relax.

When Elaine and Kim went to the mall again, Elaine took a more relaxed approach. With Kim in his stroller, they shopped first, passing Santa and watching on the sidelines as other children went up to meet him. Elaine reminded him that Santa could ho-ho-ho just like his uncle—a positive association he could now make. At the end of their excursion and holding Mom's hand, Kim stood next to Santa and spoke to him as their picture was taken. And later that day, as he stared at the photo with Santa that his mom had hung up, Kim made it known that he'd like to go back to see Santa again!

Surprising as it may sound, it's not uncommon for kids to fear someone or something that adults interpret as being fun. It could be Santa, a circus clown (talk about strange clothes and hair!), a juggler (how can tossing knives in the air be good after Mom warned about their danger?), or a magician (making people disappear or, worse, cutting them in half can be plenty frightening). Even the child's own parent in a mask for Halloween can seem shocking. The familiar becomes unfamiliar, and the child has no frame of reference to explain it. A toy can also have this effect. A two-year-old I know was reduced to tears in the face of a soft, furry, eight-inch-long, battery-operated lamb that walked and said "Baa!" Jaime would run away from it even when it was still, and the toy had to be given away because just seeing it in the back of his parents' closet terrified him. In this particular case there was no reasoning with the little boy, and the issue just wasn't important enough to bother about. Such reactions can't be predicted. The same costume or toy can strike one child as amusing and elicit fear in another, depending on each child's particular perspective, rational or not. The bottom-line solution is always the same: You can try to allay the anxiety, but if not, let it go.

Wary of Water

Every summer little Rochelle and her family rented a beach house for two weeks. Her dad and older brothers always did a little fishing while her mom kept Rochelle company on the shore. Although most of their days were spent at the beach, Rochelle never showed any inclination to join the others in the water. When she was five, her father convinced her to test the surf by wading in a few yards. He was just about to proclaim this a breakthrough occasion when Rochelle was unceremoniously knocked down by a big wave. Between sobs she proclaimed that she would never set foot in the water again. Back home, her parents asked for advice on how to turn this situation around before a winter trip to the Caribbean.

I've always felt that kids should be a little afraid of the water. I taught my own children that the water is a fine place to have a good time but they should respect it because you can get hurt. Rochelle was actually realizing the potential for an accident in the water that could cause injury. When she got knocked down and experienced a moment of panic until her father literally put her back on her feet, the water became a very real source of distress, and she developed an exaggerated fear of everything associated with the beach, even sitting on the sand. Rochelle's reeducation process emphasized the idea that "the ocean is fun, but when you're little, you must be with an adult." We then used Imagination Training with a series of rehearsals to calm Rochelle's mostly irrational fear of the water. These practice runs were in obviously safe situations, such as the tub and the wading pool in her backyard: "Close your eyes and imagine that you're sitting in your bathtub. Wiggle your toes in the water. Can you splash with your hands? That's fun, isn't it? Now think about being in your own pool on the grass outside. See your water toys? Can you pretend you're filling up your bucket with water and pouring it over your feet?"

From these familiar and secure water spaces Rochelle imagined herself sitting in a small boat while stressing its safety: "You can feel the water under the boat gently rocking, but you're safe if you hold on to the sides. The anchor is in the water, and the boat can't go anywhere. You can sit and watch the clouds making designs in the sky as long as you hold on." Once Rochelle was comfortable in this setting, she was told to imagine that the boat was drifting just a little bit while still securely attached to the dock by a strong rope. She then progressed to feeling safe outside the boat: "Now imagine you're standing next to the boat. Just your feet and ankles are in the water, and the water is nice and warm. You're holding your dad's hand, and you're going to take a little walk. You're going a little deeper, then a little deeper. The farther out you go, the nicer it feels and the more relaxed you are. Imagine that every time you take a breath, you're filling up your chest like a giant float." As part of the process, supplement the progression in the action with statements that reinforce the safety factor, such as: "As long as your face is above the water, the water can't hurt you."

After a few practice sessions, Rochelle's parents showed her the travel brochures for their upcoming trip, and Rochelle's enthusiasm started building. She began asking if her dad could take her into the water every day. And when they went through the rehearsal technique, Rochelle started to imagine the ocean in more specific terms. It became the ocean in the brochure, an excellent bridge to the real thing. On their vacation Rochelle still had some apprehension as she put her big toe into the Caribbean Sea, but her dad talked her through it as they made the same progression, step by step, that they had made during her Imagination Training practice sessions. Her parents resisted pushing her too far; they didn't rush her into taking steps she wasn't ready for, such as wading alone. The reward for everyone was that Rochelle, encouraged by her positive experience with her dad, soon started talking about taking swimming lessons at the Y to be ready for their summer vacation.

Skating on Thick Ice

A few years ago Wendy's parents bought her a pair of ice skates for her sixth birthday. Unfortunately, around the same time the family was watching a figure-skating event on television and saw a few of the competitors take some nasty falls. One skater was shown visibly grimacing in pain after her performance. Wendy decided right then and there that she would not even attempt to try out her skates no matter how much she was prodded. The skates languished in a closet until they no longer fit her. When she was eight, she was invited to a friend's birthday party, to be held at an ice-skating rink, complete with rentals and a lesson. Wendy's parents were sure she'd consent to give it a try. But the image of the skater's accident was still vivid in her mind, and she decided not to go to the party. Concerned that Wendy's fear was turning into a big issue, that she would let fear stop her from trying any athletic activity that carried some inherent risk, her parents asked if there was anything I could suggest.

Hearing how they had proceeded in their "persuasion" efforts, it was easy to see that they had helped intensify Wendy's fears. They admitted that they had laughed at her initial apprehension, insisting she was acting like a baby and almost demanding that she confront her fear of skating because this was the age, they had decided, that young girls learn to skate.

A new, less urgent strategy using Imagination Training would help Wendy get past her fear of falling. Here's what her parents suggested to her: "Imagine that you're lacing up the skates, tying them securely. Now imagine the two blades; see them getting wider and wider, almost like a platform that you can stand on. They can hold you up easily and help you glide across the ice." Next Wendy pictured herself on the ice, skating effortlessly around the rink. This is the same type of visualization technique used by professional athletes: Imagine yourself performing flawlessly to gain the confidence to go out and really do it. Where other imagination techniques draw on images that distract, in this case what works best is having Wendy concentrate on her own performance, "watching" herself do all the moves she wishes to perfect.

To save her from the inevitable bout of social insecurity that would come from making a first attempt at her friend's party, Wendy's parents agreed to take her to the rink for a lesson beforehand. Although they were both avid skaters who could certainly teach Wendy how to skate, a better idea was for this first lesson to be given by one of the rink's skating instructors. Wendy went through the visualization process once more as she laced up and knew she could recall this positive image of herself anytime she took a spill. Weeks later it was Wendy's parents who were nervous as Wendy was ready to begin attempting jumps like those she had seen on TV!

This type of sports imaging can be used to overcome a multitude of athletic fears, from solo pursuits like bike riding and skiing to team activities like playing baseball and soccer.

Hospital Heroics

Because of repeated tonsil infections, Stanley's tonsils had to be removed. Necessary hospital arrangements were made for the following week, but what immediately concerned Stanley's mother was how she should prepare him for undergoing surgery. No matter what you might say to your child, don't do it too soon. Telling your child weeks or even days in advance might find him climbing the walls by the time he's admitted, especially if your own anxiety level has been growing each day.

When talking to children about surgery and subsequent hospitalization, parents should take some time to describe the environment as best they can. Imagination Training may be helpful, but be careful, especially with younger kids. If you're not sure of the specific sequencing of hospital procedure and something occurs out of order, a child will usually focus on the one thing that wasn't as you described it, and the foundation you have carefully laid will crack. So be specific with the parts of the procedure you have relative control over and give general descriptions of those you don't. Of course, the more you can find out in advance from your pediatrician or a hospital staffer, the more exacting you can be. It's certainly more reassuring to hear "Mommy will be able to stay with you right until they start," if that's really the case.

When dealing with hospital staff, always keep an eye out for factors that might precipitate anxiety and don't feel that your hands are tied if you come up against arbitrary rules. Most people feel very intimidated in a hospital setting, but it's important to speak up if you see something happening that makes your child fearful needlessly. I often tell parents what happened to Peter, a young patient of mine who was scheduled for a minor operation.

Although his parents had explained the big picture to Peter the day before and found him very understanding of what was going to happen and calm about the proceedings, just before the operation, he was lying on a gurney in absolute hysterics. He lost control when the attendants who showed up to wheel him to the operating room forced him to take off his underpants in accordance with a somewhat archaic hospital rule. Obviously, having underwear on or off had no bearing on the surgical procedure. Fortunately, the situation was explained to a hospital administrator who allowed Peter to put his underwear back on. The change in his demeanor was instantaneous, and the procedure went off without further incident. The morale of the story: If there's something that makes a child very upset and it's not something that's written in stone, don't do it!

Following surgery of any kind, your child will undoubtedly have to cope with some degree of pain. To help Stanley get over the minor discomfort he would feel for a day or two after his tonsillectomy, a common trick used by psychologists was suggested. Stanley could visualize the pain as a big, red, glowing fireball. His mom helped him "see" it by telling him to stare at the wall in his room, and she guided his imagination: "Can you see it? It's about the size of a beach ball, round and red. Now try to shrink the ball in your mind. It's getting smaller and smaller, and its color is changing, too. It's getting darker and darker. See it go from red to dark blue, just like the ocean and the sky. Now as you make it get smaller and smaller, it will change into a little dot, and as it does, you will feel the pain less and less. And when it becomes very small, you will hardly feel it at all." If you happen to have a light on a dimmer switch, use it as a visual aid to help get your message across.

Through his own imagination, Stanley could reduce his perception of the pain from a beach ball to a little dot. The dot represents the pain that still lingers, but his pain factor would be reduced tenfold. This technique works by first giving the pain a representational quality and then reducing it to something quite manageable. We can't pretend that all discomfort will be completely gone, but it will certainly be under control—under Stanley's control. A follow-up call the next day found Stanley in good spirits and enjoying a bowl of ice cream—a useful "accessory" to calming that red fireball!

Dealing with Death

Eight-year-old Warren had an exceptionally close relationship with his grandmother. Both his parents worked outside the home, and Grandma had been his primary caregiver for as long as he could remember. One day, without any kind of warning, she had a heart attack and died. Because Warren had previously used Imagination Training for blackboard anxiety, his father wondered if there was any imagery that was especially appropriate for dealing with the grief of a death in the family.

It is generally best for parents to tell their children what they really believe about death themselves and not some fabricated story suiting the occasion. But the younger the child, the shorter the explanation should be. Avoid suggesting that Grandma "went to sleep for a long time" or "is sleeping and won't wake up." Surprisingly, rather than presenting death in a more palatable image, this explanation may actually traumatize a child and create a situation where the child is afraid to go to sleep, fearing he will never wake up. When you do decide on an explanation, you might preface it by saying, "No one really knows what happens when we die, but this is what Mommy and Daddy think." This will help avoid confusion in the event that the child is given a different version of death by someone else. As you present your views and elaborate on them, if you use either personal or religious imagery yourself, share this with your child. Many religions utilize powerful imagery and are a good source of ideas; the concepts of angels, heaven, and hell are all strong images that can be helpful to children.

Be aware, however, that certain images that you find appealing or comforting may not be thought of in the same way by your child or may be too complex for her to grasp. As is usually the case with choosing imagination themes and scenes, allowing your child to draw the figurative picture can be very effective. You can initiate the discussion by asking your child to describe his version of dying to you. Ask: "You know that Grandma was a very special person, and when she died she went to a very special place. What do you think that place looks like?" This gives your child an opportunity to clue you in on the imagery he or she finds most comfortable. You can then embellish it, making it the nicest place you can both imagine.

You might help younger children by saying, "I want you to imagine that you're taking a staircase leading to a very special place. What do you think it looks like, and where do you think it is?" Let your child decide if that staircase is going up or down; in my experience I've found that kids are pretty equally divided on whether they find up or down scary. Some are afraid of heights, while others think of down as going into a cellar with creepy-crawly things. You don't want to guess the wrong direction when asking will get you the correct answer.

Themes and Dreams: Putting It All Together

A Lexicon of Ideas for Imagination Training

THROUGHOUT THIS BOOK WE have explored a number of strategies and techniques for helping children overcome the burden of anxiety and fear. Surely childhood itself is difficult enough in our complex society, and what parent can't use a little help to make his or her child's life easier? While examples of Imagination Training themes, dreams, and scenes are sprinkled throughout, this chapter provides you with many ideas that you can draw from to create just the right imagery to appeal to your child.

Setting the Scene

Most children find it easy to drift into a fantasy world; often it is one of their own creation and it's one of their favorite forms of play. Imagination Training draws on this fantastic ability and channels it to help your child get over the rough spots. In times of stress, envisioning in the mind's eye a fabulous place can actually transport any child far away from his or her anxieties. The range of activities that can be explored and developed are limited only by your and your child's imagination. I've frequently discussed the added value of having your child suggest the themes that appeal to him. It makes the theme easier to imagine and more enjoyable, and therefore more effective. And of course the most effective ones can be used over and over again.

Some children do best if they focus first on an object or a sound to tune out their surroundings. Others can do better by entering directly into an imaginative thought. To get your child to initiate the setting, start him off by saying, "Imagine a favorite place you have been or where you would like to be. See and feel yourself in a place that makes you feel happy, a place without any problems. Remember how good it feels to be in a place like that? I'll bet you can feel that good right now."

It is not only visual imagery that comes into play as your child travels to a fantasy environment, but also sounds, smells, and movements. These details make the experience come alive. Try to include all the components of the particular environment you want him to envision. The more elements that are included, the greater his or her involvement will be. The most effective "daydreams" often occur when the child and parent can adapt the setting and actions to the child's individual interests, past experience, and personality.

Some parents worry that they are not creative enough to make interesting or believable scenes. Others worry that under pressure or in an emergency they'll be too stressed to help distract their child from the immediate problem. Remember that the distraction of helping your child also helps you, the parent, to calm down, too. I have found that there are many more parents who worry about their performance than those who actually "fail" at Imagination Training. Nonetheless, here are some of the most popular settings. Use them "as is" or as a guide for developing a special place that you and your child will choose. The idea is for you to describe colors, shapes, and sounds so that your child can imagine the environment with all of his senses, and then to ask your child to join in.

Favorite Places

1. Place: A Garden of Eden

Components: a warm, sunny day; favorite flowers in special colors; wonderful aromas; birds singing and bees buzzing; a quiet pool; a soft breeze; shade under the trees; a blanket to sit on.

Activities: enjoying a picnic, picking a bouquet of flowers, taking a nap in the sun, collecting tadpoles in the pond, finding colorful leaves, watching a spider spin its web.

2. Place: A Carnival, Amusement Park, or County Fair

Components: rides such as a roller coaster and Ferris wheel, people dressed in costumes, flashing lights, ringing bells, colorful tents, booths with games to play and their shelves of prizes, calliope music from the carousel, sounds of laughter, shouts from the carnival hawkers, aromas of hot dogs and cotton candy.

Activities: going on each ride, taking a pony ride, petting some animals, eating some of your favorite foods, winning a prize by throwing darts, watching a performance, laughing as you walk through the funhouse.

3. Place: The Beach

Components: the sight and sound of waves breaking; a blue sky, hot sun, and clouds drifting by; seagulls in the air; the sand, colorful umbrellas, and blankets; a favorite towel and bathing suit; sand toys and sunglasses; sailboats going by; people swimming and shouting; the salty smell; the boardwalk; a lifeguard station.

Activities: riding a wave, collecting shells, playing Frisbee, having a picnic, listening to the radio, taking a nap, walking along the shore, building sand castles, burying Dad's legs in the sand, floating on a raft, fishing from a pier, digging a deep hole, catching a crab.

4. Place: A Pirate Ship

Components: a three-masted sailing ship with a skull-and-crossbones flag and billowing sails, pirates with eyepatches and striped shirts, the captain with a peg leg and a parrot on his shoulder, a lookout high in the crow's nest, the gleaming cannon, a chest filled with jewels, a secret treasure map, the creaking and rocking of the ship, dropping the anchor, the salty air, dolphins swimming alongside.

Activities: searching for an island, then exploring it; putting up the sails; steering the ship; firing the cannon at another ship; deckside sword fights; fishing for food; following signs on the treasure map; digging for the treasure chest, finding the loot, and dividing it.

5. Place: A Stadium

Components: rows of colored seats, the enthusiastic crowd, athletes (choose the sport) in their different uniforms warming up on the field, vendors selling food, the flashing scoreboard, music and the sounds of clapping and cheering and the public-address announcer, the smell of popcorn and other favorite foods.

Activities: eating a hotdog and peanuts as you cheer on your team; becoming one of the players; catching a foul ball, dunking a basketball, kicking a goal, scoring a touchdown, or hitting a home run; winning the game or a medal for your team after making a key play; talking to the famous players; seeing your family in the crowd; being interviewed on TV.

6. Place: A Theater

Components: the marquee, the stage, rows of seats, the balcony, and glistening chandeliers; an orchestra noisily tuning up; people arriving all dressed up and taking their seats; ushers with flashlights; the rising curtain; colored spotlights; actors in fancy costumes with sparkling jewelry; singing and dancing.

Activities: listening to the performance of your favorite singer or band or watching a performance of your favorite story (*Cinderella,*

Beauty and the Beast, Sleeping Beauty); joining the performance—singing a song, tap dancing, pirouetting in a ballet, acting in a play, playing an instrument or leading a rock band, doing magic tricks, telling jokes and stories, wearing a special costume with fancy makeup; putting on a puppet show; doing tricks with your pet.

7. Place: A Holiday or Party

Components: all your relatives and friends mingling; a room specially decorated with balloons and glittering streamers; a table filled with brightly wrapped presents; a beautiful fancy cake; bowls of favorite foods, candies, and treats.

Activities: watching a special performer present a show, opening your presents, singing songs, eating favorite foods, playing party games.

Some other adventures that might stimulate a child's imagination are visiting the zoo, a Wild West rodeo, a dinosaur park, the circus, or a firehouse; a ride in the space shuttle; a trip in a submarine, going on a jungle safari, or camping; living in a castle or under the sea; flying in a balloon; or floating on a cloud. When you see that your child is particularly intrigued by a place or adventure or something he saw in a movie or on a TV show that made him feel good, jot down the particulars. Then turn the idea into a theme anytime the need arises. Above all, don't be afraid to try something new.

Getting There

Images involving transportation can often help a child get to a happier time or place. The common denominator with all these "vehicles" is that they come equipped with a built-in control mechanism that allows your child to decide where, when, and how. Begin the suggestion by offering a real and familiar vehicle (plane, train, and so forth) and "modify" it to put it at your child's commands. Figuring out which mode of transportation your youngster likes and enjoys is not hard if you begin with the following question and follow-up suggestions: "What would you like to take a ride in the best? . . . Great idea! Now just get comfortable and imagine you are in it right now. Remember that you are in control. . . . You can go wherever you want to and as fast or as slow as you like. When you get to the spot where you want to be, just slow down and land softly." Enhance the experience by having your child notice all the things that pass by. She can go out of her way to view special things she has always wanted to see and even take along friends to make it more fun.

Favorite Vehicles

1. Vehicle: Airplane

Control mechanism: the instrument panel controlled by the pilot who decides on speed and direction. (Another option is having a special parachute that allows him to land softly wherever he chooses.)

2. Vehicle: Boat

Control mechanism: Put your child in complete control by making him captain at the helm. Steering with the wheel or rudder allows freedom to travel anywhere. A special button releases an anchor that eases the boat into the dock.

3. Vehicle: Car

Control mechanism: A special magic key turns on the ignition and puts the steering wheel at your child's command. Simple pressure on the brake stops the car at whatever destination is chosen.

4. Vehicle: Magic Carpet

Control mechanism: Like a genie's, your child's voice controls the altitude and destination; a magic word will make the carpet land gently.

5. Vehicle: Bicycle

Control mechanism: While pedaling, pulling up on the handlebars sends the bicycle upward. Applying the brakes lands the bicycle anywhere.

These vehicles will take your child as far as his imagination allows. In fact, let his imagination determine just how exotic his mode of transportation can be, from in-line skates or a skateboard to a majestic Arabian stallion, an elephant, or a camel.

Great Escapes

Distraction is great for redirecting a child's attention away from something unpleasant to something fun. Distraction techniques such as blowing bubbles and showing pop-up books work especially well for younger children. But that doesn't mean distraction is reserved for little kids, just that the methods must keep up with your child's development. The following games do just that; they require concentration rather than a great imagination. They are simple, straightforward, and very distracting. If your child has special or specific interests, tailor these games accordingly.

Distraction Activities

1. Math Games

Simple exercises that your child's teacher will love to have you suggest include counting forward and backward, practicing multiplying (2 times 2 times 2 . . .) or adding (2 plus 2 plus 2 . . .), and counting things in your immediate surroundings (flowers on the wallpaper, tiles on the floor, cracks in the ceiling).

2. Name Games

These include having your child spell the names of all her friends and relatives; naming all the players on a sports team or naming all the teams in a sports league; naming and spelling (depending on age) all the animals in the jungle, all the states in the United States, all the foods in your refrigerator, all the toys in her closet.

3. Guessing Games
Give a description of a familiar person, toy, or animal and have the child guess who or what it is.

4. Reverse Spelling
Pick words your child can spell and ask him to spell them backward.

Two's Company

The Takealong Friend is a core concept that is appropriate for countless fears. But don't feel that you are limited to Superman and his fellow superheroes. Any favorite character is capable of protecting your child and can be pressed into service. When your child is engrossed in fantasizing about one of these characters, it's easy to suggest that he or she become an active participant in the daydream. It is also possible to hold these characters up as role models who exhibit the kind of behavior your child is trying to master. If you've ever noticed how children sit immobilized in front of a TV set, you know how easily they merge themselves into the show. Memorable shows or stories are often acted out repeatedly over time, either in their minds or with dolls at playtime. That's why the concept works so well at "stress time," too. In case you're not aware of the current pop-culture heroes, most children have a ready list to offer.

While characters go in and out of vogue at an alarming pace, many have endured for generations. Some come from the ranks of morning TV, others from popular movies, and a few from the comics. To find the perfect Takealong Friend, ask your child to name favorite characters from books he's familiar with. Ask the school-age child, "Is there a famous person you've heard about in school that you would like to be?" The following list includes characters who have stood the test of time as well as some of the most popular newcomers.

Takealong Friends: Heroes and Heroines

Ariel from Disney's *The Little Mermaid*

Barney and Baby Bop

Batman and Robin

Belle from Disney's *Beauty and the Beast*

Big Bird, Snuffy, Bert, Ernie, and the other "Sesame Street" characters

Charlie Brown and Snoopy

Clifford the Dog

Dorothy and Toto from *The Wizard of Oz*

Garfield

Genie (*Aladdin*)

Gerbert

Lamb Chop, Hush Puppy, and Charlie Horse

Little Rascals

Madeline

Mighty Max

Mighty Morphin Power Rangers

Rocky and Bullwinkle

Speed Racer

Teenage Mutant Ninja Turtles

Thomas the Tank Engine and Mr. Conductor (*Shining Time Station*)

X-Men

Epilogue: Getting Started

EVEN AFTER READING THIS book, some parents may doubt their ability to share Imagination Training techniques with their child or may worry that when the time comes to try "IT" out, it won't come naturally to them or to their son or daughter. If this happens, remember the essential simplicity of Imagination Training; it is simply teaching your child to use his own imagination to accomplish something that he wouldn't otherwise be able to. Remember, too, that imagination or fantasy play comes naturally to almost every child.

Try to find one area that does feel natural to you and decide ahead of time what you're going to say, then broaden the theme as you go along. Maybe the Cloud Copter is easy for you to picture and describe, or maybe a more "concrete" figure like Superman— one you've been familiar with for decades—will work better for you. You'll be surprised to find that if you plant even the smallest seed or image in your child's mind, she will make it grow.

If you're reluctant to try "IT" because you feel it isn't truthful— a penny can't really bring you luck after all, you say—think of "IT" as a source of encouragement for your child rather than a lie, the same as Santa Claus and the tooth fairy. Regarding time constraints, taking a little time to teach one of these techniques will actually save time in the long run, time that would be lost if your child's anxiety continued and you used unsuccessful "reasoning" to help him or her get over the fear. And it can't be said often enough: It will take longer to read the description of an "IT" theme than to actually suggest it to your child! To help you overcome your own apprehensions about trying Imagination Training, follow this three-step approach when you want to introduce "IT":

1. Let your first sentence create an atmosphere of trust to both calm and reassure a frightened child: "I know that you are feeling upset" or "This can sure seem scary."
2. Next, introduce the idea of finding a solution: "Let's see what we can do about this problem" or "I bet if we think about it, we can find a way to fix this."
3. Present your message in a comforting, hopeful way: "I've heard that using a special pen and holding it the right way will help you pass your test at school. Why don't we try it out?"

You'll find that once you introduce the suggestion, your child will seize on it. Give him the pen, and he will quickly feel its empowerment.

Do remember that different strategies work better at different times. Using directive language tends to be most helpful for stressful situations: If your child is very upset, try the firm "I'm going to help you." If it's not a crisis situation, choose the more easygoing "it'll be interesting to see what happens" approach.

While we've tried to address many of the difficult passages children face as they grow, you might find your child in a dilemma not covered in this book. Keep in mind that Imagination Training can be used to overcome almost any type of problem, from decreasing anxiety and controlling pain to easing phobias and changing behaviors. Many pediatricians have found ways to incorporate these ideas to help kids overcome nail biting, thumb sucking, and bedwetting. "IT" is worth discussing with your child's doctor if you need advice for these very common problems. The great thing about Imagination Training is that, like imagination itself, it has no boundaries. There are no limits to what you can use "IT" to achieve.

For Further Reading

H. Benson. *The Relaxation Response*. New York: Morrow. 1975.

D. D. Brigham, *Imagery for Getting Well: Clinical Applications of Behavioral Medicine*. New York: W. W. Norton & Co., 1994.

C. M. Citrenbaum, et al. *Modern Clinical Hypnosis for Habit Control*. New York: W. W. Norton & Co., 1985.

D. C. Hammond, ed. *Handbook of Hypnotic Suggestions and Metaphors*. New York: W. W. Norton & Co., 1990.

J. R. Hilgard and S. LeBaron. *Hypnotherapy of Pain in Children with Cancer*. Los Altos, Cal.: William Kaufmann, Inc., 1984.

K. Olness, ed. "Biofeedback Therapy." *Pediatric Annals*, March 1991.

K. Olness and G. Gardner. *Hypnosis and Hypnotherapy with Children*. Philadelphia, Pa.: Grune and Stratton, 1988.

W. C. Wester and D. J. O'Grady, eds. *Clinical Hypnosis with Children*. New York: Brunner/Mazel Publishers, 1991.

R. P. Zahourek. *Relaxation and Imagery: Tools for Therapeutic Communication and Intervention*. Philadelphia, Pa.: W. B. Saunders Co., 1988.

Index

SONG OF SEDNA

SONG OF SEDNA

adapted by Robert D. San Souci

illustrated by Daniel San Souci

DOUBLEDAY
NEW YORK   LONDON   TORONTO   SYDNEY   AUCKLAND

To our parents

Published by Doubleday, a division of
Bantam Doubleday Dell Publishing Group, Inc.
666 Fifth Avenue, New York, New York 10103

Doubleday and the portrayal of an anchor with a dolphin
are trademarks of Doubleday, a division of
Bantam Doubleday Dell Publishing Group, Inc.

Library of Congress Cataloging-in-Publication Data
San Souci, Robert.
Song of Sedna.
SUMMARY: Retells one of many versions of how an
Eskimo maiden became goddess of the sea.
1. Eskimos—Legends.   [1. Eskimos—Legends]
I. San Souci, Daniel.   II. Title.
E99.E7S316   398.2′08997 [E]   80-627
ISBN 0-385-24823-7 (pbk.)

2 4 6 8 10 9 7 5 3

According to Eskimo myth, Sedna is the
goddess of the sea who aids fishermen
and hunters.

This book tells one of the many versions
of the story of how an Eskimo maiden was
transformed into the goddess of the sea.

In the old days, when people were different than they are now, a young Eskimo woman named Sedna lived beside the Arctic Ocean. She was the only daughter of Noato the hunter, whose wife had died when Sedna was born.

Sedna was so beautiful that young men came from near and far to court her. But she was attracted to none of them, and so she refused to marry.

"You must choose a husband soon, my daughter," her father warned, "before word of your fickleness keeps all the young men away."

Sedna answered, "One day the man I have seen in my dreams will come for me. I will not refuse him."

The old man Noato simply shook his head and despaired that his daughter would ever marry. Sedna was strong-willed; more so than her father, whose courage often failed him.

While Sedna waited for the man who was to be her husband, she often wandered with her husky, Setka, who had the blood of the wolf in him. She had raised him from a pup.

Then one day a handsome young hunter arrived from a far-off land. He was dressed in splendid furs and carried a harpoon carved from a single whalebone. The prow of his umiak was unlike those of Sedna's people: It was carved like the head of a serpent.

"My name is Mattak," the stranger said. "Word of your beauty has reached my homeland. Come away with me and be my bride."

Though Sedna recognized him as the man she had dreamed about, she hesitated, for it seemed, as he spoke, that clouds suddenly raced across the sky and a chilling wind arose out of nowhere to whisper a warning in her ear.

Her dog, Setka, broke his tether and ran away.

"What will you offer me to leave my father's igloo behind?" she asked.

He answered, "You shall be mistress of my home on the Island of Birds. There the lamp is always filled with oil, and the pot, with meat."

Sedna was excited by the stranger's promises, but she wished her father was not away hunting so that he could advise her.

"I will give you necklaces of ivory," Mattak continued, "and warm bearskins to rest on. The birds will wake you gently and sing you to sleep."

Feeling as though she moved in a dream, Sedna put aside her doubts and held out her hand to her suitor. With a cry of joy he grasped it and led her toward his umiak, which sat like a giant gull on the shore.

Sedna wished to take her dog with her, but though she called and called, Setka would not return.

She was sad to leave her home behind, but Mattak was anxious to depart. Together they set out across the cloudy and wind-tossed sea.

When Noato returned home, he saw the umiak in the distance. He turned away because the sight grieved him so. He feared that he would never again see his only child.

Sedna and the hunter paddled for five days across a sea grown dark and strange. Sedna often found herself thinking that she had been moving—and continued to move—in a dream. Her companion spoke hardly at all. For much of the time Sedna had only the sound of the wind, the distant cry of birds, and the splash of the waves against the hull to keep her company.

On the sixth day, they entered a harbor guarded by giant polar bears. Sedna was frightened by the beasts, but Mattak told her not to be afraid. His voice calmed her, so that even when one bear reared back and roared, Sedna did not cry out.

They landed in a place where flocks of birds wheeled overhead and thronged the shores and covered the cliff faces in robes of feathered bodies. It seemed to Sedna that the very sun was darkened by the number of birds.

Sedna was amazed to discover that Mattak's home was merely a cave amid the tumbled stones and snow.

Using the snow knife she had brought with her, Sedna showed her husband how to carve out heavy blocks of ice and build a proper igloo. They packed the cracks between the blocks with snow to keep the wind out and bored a hole in the topmost ice block to let warm air escape.

True to his word, Mattak supplied his new wife with more hides and food than she had ever seen before.

She scraped and tanned the skins and gathered soft feathers from the bird cliffs to line the garments she sewed.

Sedna's life was rich and comfortable, but there were times when, alone at her sewing, she became as troubled as the winds and shadows that plagued this otherwise peaceful land.

There came a day when Mattak went on a hunt and forgot his lucky amulet, a bit of ivory carved like a raven's foot.

Sedna followed for a long time in the direction her husband had gone. As she rounded an outcropping of rock and ice, Sedna saw her husband a little way ahead of her. Suddenly she drew back and hid as she saw him change shape. Mattak grew huge wings and soared into the sky. Instantly she knew the truth: She had wed a bird-spirit, an enchanted being who could sometimes take human form.

The young woman fled back to her igloo in fear and confusion. Haunted by the knowledge that she had married a nonhuman, she wept and wondered what to do.

Meanwhile, her father, Noato, who had grown increasingly lonely, had decided to follow his daughter to the Island of Birds. He called his friend the angakok, shaman, who put a blessing on Noato's umiak and told the old man a magic formula to keep his boat safe.

After a long journey, Noato, who had nearly fainted with terror as he passed the huge polar bears, arrived on the island. He found his daughter, filled with grief, pacing the shore. When Sedna told him her husband's secret, Noato insisted that she come away with him.

Sedna agreed this was the best plan, so they put out to sea as quickly as possible, for they were both fearful of the wrath of her demon-husband.

When Mattak returned and discovered that his wife had fled, at first he wept and raged, then he set out in pursuit. His anger and his demon strength enabled him to paddle swiftly through the water.

Soon he came within shouting distance of Noato's boat and cried, "Return Sedna to me!"

Sedna and Noato refused to listen and kept paddling. Then Mattak transformed his own umiak into a huge sea serpent with demon-fire blasting from its jaws.

The angakok's blessing and the magic words Noato had learned kept them always a little ahead of the pursuing monster.

When he saw that he could not overtake them, Mattak gave a tremendous cry of rage. The father and daughter, fearfully looking back, saw a huge bird-shape astride the dragon. Then Mattak's immense wings spread across the sky. Noato and Sedna dared look no longer, but put all their strength into their rowing.

The beating of the giant wings was like thunder. The huge body of the bird blackened the sky like massed storm clouds. There came a shrill cry which grew into the sound of a terrifying storm sweeping across the ocean.

Noato repeated his magic formula, but it was less effective now, because magic loses its power by being used. Seeing this, Noato's courage failed him utterly.

The wind boomed around the tiny boat; waves, rising up, clamored, "Return Sedna to us!"

Convinced that he had offended spirits of sea and storm, Noato hurled his daughter from the boat as a sacrifice to quiet the unearthly voices howling on all sides.

Three times Sedna attempted to climb back into the boat, and each time her fainthearted father pushed her away, crying, "We have offended very great spirits. They call you back, and I must make peace with them."

Exhausted, finally, Sedna gave up the struggle and sank down to the bottom of the sea. A powerful blessing was on her, so she was able to breathe water as if it were air and walk across the floor of the sea as if she were still on dry land.

Two banded seals came and swam above her. In voices as soft as their furred skin, they told her, "Approach that mountain and you will find your destiny."

Sedna guessed that these were really seal-spirits, so she set out toward a mountain of blue ice and ivory in the distance.

On her way she crossed a part of the Kingdom of the Dead. Ghostly shapes on all sides urged her to forsake her journey and rest with them.

"Close your ears," advised the first seal-spirit.

"Your destiny lies ahead of you," the other said.

Sedna drew upon her inner strength and ignored the ghost-voices that called out to her to join them.

Suddenly Sedna encountered a killer whale so ferocious-looking she cried out, "Alas!" and stopped.

But her spirit-guides urged her forward.

The first said, "Have courage."

And the second told her, "Climb upon his back, and he will carry you toward the mountain."

Though she was afraid, she made herself take a step toward the whale. The creature twisted and watched her with eyes as cold as ice chips, but it made no move to attack her.

She put a hand out and discovered that the whale's skin was as ridged as the face of a very old person. Using her hands and feet she climbed onto the back of the beast, which then rose from the sea floor so swiftly that the girl thought she would be swept off as the water rushed past.

The whale carried her most of the way to the mountain, but stopped at the edge of a huge abyss. Across the bottomless canyon arched a bridge as slender as a knife blade.

"This is the last task," said one seal-spirit.

"You must cross the bridge on foot," said the other.

Balancing carefully, Sedna made her way across the delicate bridge, which ended some distance away from the mountain and high above the sea floor.

Urged by the seal-spirits, she swam down and reached the mountain of blue ice and ivory. There she found a throne waiting for her on the highest peak.

All the creatures of the sea gathered around her—walruses, whales, seals, and a multitude of fish—and they proclaimed her goddess of the sea. They promised to obey her every command.

When Sedna was seated upon the throne on the mountain peak, the seal-spirits swam up to her.

The first said to her, "Now anything you wish is in your power."

"But use your power wisely," the second warned, "for a god uses power tempered by wisdom and mercy."

Sedna realized that she was being tested. She sensed that her powers might be taken from her if she misused them. So she followed the best instincts of her heart.

She moved her hands, and power flowed from them. She became, for a moment, one with the waters and caused them to swallow up the igloo where her father lay sleeping near her dog, Setka.

When the old man and dog had been pulled beneath the waves, the seal-spirits brought them before Sedna, who had returned to her throne upon the mountain.

Noato trembled to see the change in his daughter, for her power shone all around her. He was sure she would punish him for having thrown her from the boat so heartlessly.

But Sedna, who felt the force and rightness of her destiny, forgave her father and made a home for him in the land beneath the sea. She made Setka special guardian of her throne.

Her actions pleased Silarssuaq, the great spirit of justice, who is the most powerful being of all.

From the bottom of the Arctic Ocean, Sedna reigns to this day as goddess of the sea. The Eskimos seek her goodwill whenever they need protection on the open sea or help with harvesting the sea's bounty.

They say that sometimes, when the sea wind blows a certain way, you can hear the voice of Sedna singing:

> "My joy
> Rises from the depths of the sea like bubbles
> That burst in the light;
> My song
> Is a promise for the winds to carry
> To everyone who lives by the sea."

Robert D. San Souci is a graduate in English Literature from St. Mary's College in California and has written many articles and short stories for journals and magazines in the San Francisco Bay Area. He is now living in Berkeley, California, where he works in a publishing company.

Daniel San Souci, like his brother, was born in California and graduated from the California College of Arts and Crafts. His paintings have won numerous awards, and his work is on display in various galleries and in private collections. He now lives in Oakland, California.

SONG OF SEDNA is the San Soucis' second book for Doubleday. Their first, <u>The Legend of Scarface</u>, was named by the New York <u>Times Book Review</u> as one of the Ten Best Illustrated Children's Books of 1978.

The Spanish
ARMADA

Panorama of History Series
This series has been created to provide a vivid portrayal of major events in world history. Each text is concise but authoritative, giving essential facts combined with an insight into the character of the period and people involved. Every book includes a large number of full-colour illustrations and many more in black and white all researched from contemporary sources; these paintings, prints, maps and photographs all carry informative captions and are carefully integrated with the text. Other titles already published are **The Battle of Trafalgar, Last of the Tsars** and **The Industrial Revolution.** Further 'Panoramas' will be added to the series at regular intervals.

Panorama of History Series

The Spanish ARMADA

Christopher Falkus

 Pan Books Ltd : London

Published 1972 by Pan Books Ltd,
33 Tothill Street, London SW1.

ISBN 0 330 02992 4

(c) Marshall Cavendish U.S.A. Limited, 1972.

The material contained in this book is based on material
first published in 'History Makers'.

This book may not be sold in the United States of America or Canada.

Printed by Proost, Turnhout, Belgium.

Picture Credits

Contents

The Confrontation

Undoubtedly Elizabeth of England and Philip of Spain wanted to remain friends. Why was it then that England was forced to take on the might of the Spanish Empire? Why was the Spanish king prepared to launch the biggest fleet that Europe had ever seen to crush this defiant island?

A view of London in the 16th century, with London Bridge, centre. London was the heart of activity in Elizabethan England and one of the most glittering capitals of the age. It was a staunchly Protestant city and the loyalty of its militia provided a firm framework of security during the early troubled years of Elizabeth's reign.

In the spring of 1588 the shipyards of Spain were busy. In the well-guarded harbour of Lisbon a fleet was assembling for the invasion of England. Along the coastlines of Cornwall and Devon anxious eyes watched the horizon for a line of masts that would mean the beginning of the battle for England. Everybody knew that a clash of nations was at hand: and also of creeds. For Spain and England represented that cleavage between Catholic and Protestant which had divided peoples and governments since the Reformation. And in their chapels the rulers of both countries, Philip II and Elizabeth I, prayed to the same God that in the coming trial righteousness would prevail.

The year 1588 was more than a year of destiny in international politics and in the history of religion. It was also a moment of truth in two great lives, each, by the standards of the time, approaching old age. Though in many ways obvious contrasts, both Philip and Elizabeth had already laboured beyond the normal 16th century life span for fundamentally similar ends – to unify their nations in a period of unprecedented upheaval and change. To this task they brought personalities innately cautious rather than reckless, conservative rather than radical. Neither would willingly hazard the future on the fortunes of war. Yet now these ageing sovereigns, who in happier times could have been, if not friends, then allies, and perhaps man and wife, were preparing for a showdown which neither wanted and which in a very real sense itself represented the collapse of their hopes.

By virtue of the sheer extent of his domains Philip must be regarded as the chief figure of his age. He was not only King of Spain, but also ruler of the Spanish Empire in the New World, including the silver-rich lands of Peru and Mexico. He ruled

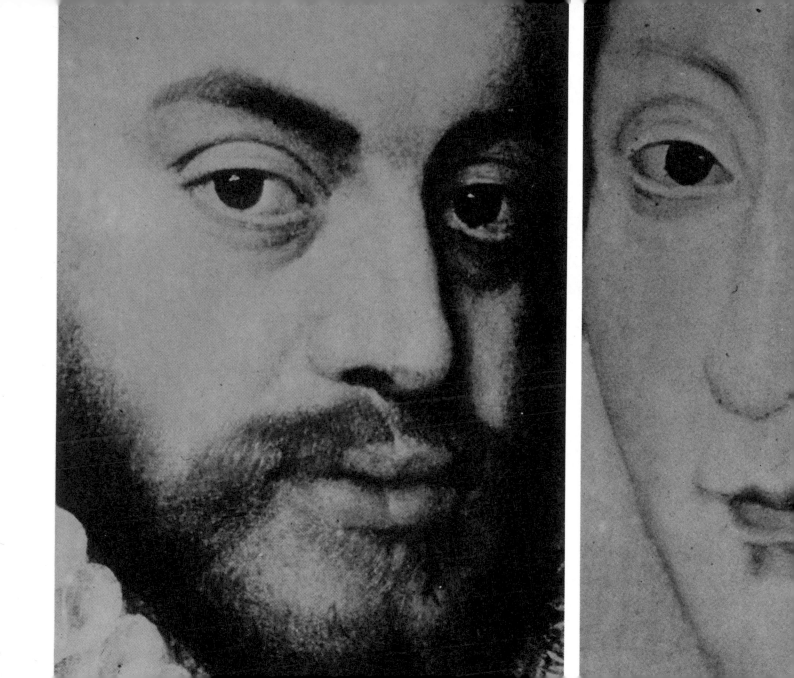

Milan, Naples, Sicily, and the Spanish Netherlands which correspond to present-day Belgium and Holland; and in 1580 he laid claim to Portugal and the Portuguese Empire in Brazil, West Africa, Ceylon, and the Indies. He thus became lord of the first empire on which the sun never set, though there is little evidence that he found much joy in his position. His portraits reveal a man of earnest, brooding seriousness: his large Habsburg jaw lends him an air of perpetual sorrow rather than resolution. His personal habits were austere, and he seems to have by-passed any period of youthful exuberance such as Henry VIII exploited to the full. Indeed, compared with most of his contemporaries, and despite an undeserved reputation for immorality, he rarely took advantage of the sexual delights which were almost the birthright of Renaissance monarchs. Instead of pleasure Philip bent himself to his Faith and to the minute administration of his colossal empire. He built for this purpose the forbidding, fortress-like Escorial – serving as a palace and a monastery; with his intended tomb at its heart. There he laboured day in, day out, minuting in his own hand the margins of the mountains of State papers presented to him. One diplomat, knowing Philip's passion for detail, referred in a dispatch to a stain he had noticed on a window. On this dispatch, in Philip's own hand, is the comment 'probably a fly' – a symbol of, or perhaps a monument to, infinite patience, care, and also fatal narrow-mindedness.

For Philip, despite his superhuman – almost *in*human – qualities, was not a great ruler. He was too detached, too lacking in passion. He could wonder about stains on the window, but never wonder whether the policies he pursued with dogged thoroughness were the right ones. He had a degree of inflexibility, of certainty, which is the antithesis of statesmanship. In seeking to promote uniformity among his subjects he did not pause to ask whether there was a solution other than complete outward and inward obedience to himself and his Church. Where heresy raised its head he sought to consume it in the cleansing fires of the Inquisition; not in a spirit of hatred, but secure in the knowledge that it was God's will that heretics be sent to a higher judge without delay, in their own interests as well as those of the empire whose religious conformity he was striving to preserve.

If Philip is easy to picture as the stern, implacable spirit of militant Catholicism, Elizabeth is far less easy to assess as the

The Catholic and Protestant champions, Philip and Elizabeth.

A contempory print showing a massacre of Dutch Protestants by the Spanish. Philip's policy of religious persecution was pursued with spectacular and bloodthirsty zeal by his governor general, the Duke of Alva, and led to outright rebellion under the Dutch flag of William the Silent. The city of Haarlem was starved into surrender by Alva's son Frederick, who continued his father's brutal round of torture and execution. Spanish tyranny in the Netherlands led to conflict with England.

12

HAERLEM

Protestant champion. Her personal religious beliefs themselves are largely a matter for speculation because, while it would be wrong to assume she did not hold them deeply, she knew how to keep them to herself. She had to. As the daughter of Anne Boleyn she was the living symbol of Henry VIII's break with Rome. Before Elizabeth's accession she had witnessed a violent swing towards Protestantism during the short lifetime of her half-brother Edward VI and then a bloody reaction in favour of Rome under her half-sister Mary Tudor (daughter of Katharine of Aragon), who had burned Protestants at the stake. As Mary tried to extirpate heresy by fire Elizabeth had become a natural focus of hope for those Protestants who either lay low during the Terror or temporarily exiled themselves to the Continent. Clearly in this period Elizabeth was in permanent danger. Her survival, if Mary remained childless, threatened the Catholic future. Not surprisingly she found herself in the Tower, and while there must often have wondered if she would ever be given her freedom again. But when at last Mary died Elizabeth, at twenty-five, mature beyond her years and wise in the ways of the world, ascended the throne to the undisguised relief of those who wished to get on once more with the process of Reformation.

Cautious diplomacy

What sort of woman was this young Queen, opening her reign in such testing circumstances? The question is not easy to answer, nor was it for her contemporaries. All her life Elizabeth remained something of an enigma, and in many vital moments of her reign her motives and intentions were obscure. Her subjects wondered why she never married, implored her to name her successor and, time and time again, demanded a firmer line against the Catholics. They could not understand her, and nor fully can we. But despite their perplexity, her subjects grew to love her, and she them, in a way that lends her reign many of the characteristics of a protracted love-affair – including the lovers' quarrels. For Elizabeth knew how to fight for what she wanted, sometimes in a furious rage, sometimes with the answerless answer: 'I will not in so deep a matter wade with so shallow a wit,' she once told the House of Commons who had pressed her to take a husband. And sometimes, of course, she could use the advantage of her sex to plead, weep a little, and win sympathy for the weakness of a mere woman in a world of men. Yet in the end Elizabeth asserted herself triumphantly in the world of men, and

Left: Mary, Queen of Scots, was an unfortunate, but vital pawn in a bitter, violent political game. The grand-daughter of Margaret, sister of Henry VIII, who had married James IV of Scotland, she was considered by Catholics to be the legitimate heir to the English throne. **Right:** *William the Silent, prince of Orange, was the leader of the Netherlands in its long struggle for independence against Spain. He did not live to see his dream accomplished, and for diplomatic reasons Elizabeth never pledged him England's full support.*

The triumphant entry of Mary I with the Princess Elizabeth into London in 1553. Mary, the daughter of Henry VIII and Katharine of Aragon, ascended the throne on Edward VI's death. An ardent Catholic, her five-year reign was a black period for Protestants, over 300 of whom were burned at the stake. Her marriage to Philip II of Spain made him joint sovereign of England for a brief time but Catholic hopes were dashed when Mary died childless.

not a little of this triumph lay in the love she inspired, and gave, to her people. As she said to her Commons: 'Though you have had and may have many mightier and wiser Princes, yet you never had and shall never have one that will love you better.'

This glorious epitaph to her reign bears little relation to the uneasy period which followed her accession. If her early years had been dangerous she found it no easier to declare herself – and her religion – once she was Queen. The experiences of the broad mass of her people under Mary had no doubt diminished their enthusiasm for Rome. But there is no evidence that the majority wished to stop being 'catholic' in matters of basic doctrine and worship. This was an attitude which Elizabeth shared. From what we know of her own views she was conservative, liked ceremony, wanted to keep the Church hierarchy, but was committed to some kind of dissociation from Rome. Thus, she took the title 'supreme governor of the Church in England' though for tactical reasons she tried at first to keep her relations with the Papacy as harmonious as possible.

But Elizabeth's views on Church matters were not nearly radical enough for many of her subjects. These included those exiles from Mary's reign who had streamed back from the Continent on the joyful news of Elizabeth's accession and who expected great things from the daughter of Anne Boleyn. Such men wanted not only to purify Church *doctrine* but also Church *government*; and Elizabeth would not give way beyond a certain point. The result was the famous 'compromise' between Elizabeth and her fervent, patriotic Puritan opponents, who yet proved her staunchest supporters when the enemy was Popish. By this compromise England got a Church which was Catholic in ceremony, but without the Mass and the Pope. However, the doctrine was distinctly Puritan in tone.

Though the Puritans proved an immediate problem, the Catholics were remarkably quiet for the first decade of the reign. Elizabeth refused to make martyrs, and hoped that a combination of convenience and apathy would induce England's Catholics to conform. She nearly succeeded. Catholicism gradually lost ground until it survived, almost as a social institution, primarily in the great inaccessible country-houses of the North Country. Then, in 1568, something happened to transform the situation. An English priest, Cardinal Allen, had decided that unless Catholicism was reinforced immediately, it would wither and die in England. He therefore founded a missionary college at

William Cecil, Lord Burghley was Elizabeth's chief minister for fourteen years and responsible for originating and directing much of her policy. In religious affairs he pursued a prudent middle course but his overriding concern was to see England supreme among the great powers of Europe. Theirs was a brilliant partnership and he remained a valued counsellor until his death at the age of 78.

Douai to train priests specifically for the task of reconversion. In 1570 he managed to have Elizabeth excommunicated by the Pope. She was declared 'to be deprived of her pretended title of the kingdom . . . and of all dominion, dignity and privilege whatsoever; and also the nobility, subjects, and people of the said kingdom, and all others who have in any sort sworn unto her, to be for ever absolved from any such oath, and all manner of duty of dominion, allegiance and obedience.' This was tantamount to a declaration of war by the Catholic Church against the Elizabethan State. Philip, as the leading Catholic sovereign, found it difficult to stand aloof from it, and it was certainly to play a part in hardening his resolve to act against Elizabeth when political differences later brought them into open confrontation. How this confrontation came about was the result of one of the most fundamental revolutions in English diplomatic history.

At the beginning of her reign Elizabeth probably never envisaged war with Spain. England was then in fact at war with her hereditary enemy, France. She had been so on and off for the last 250 years. She would be so for the next 250 years.

Elizabeth's relationship with France was also complicated by the problem of Mary Queen of Scots. Mary was the granddaughter of the sister of Henry VIII. In Catholic eyes this gave her a better claim to the English throne than Elizabeth, the daughter of Anne Boleyn, whom Henry had married after divorcing his first wife, Katharine of Aragon. The Catholic Church refused to regard this divorce as valid, and therefore saw Elizabeth as illegitimate and so ineligible to succeed to the throne. Mary was married to the heir to the French throne, and so France had an obvious reason for supporting Mary's claim to be the true Queen of England.

But peace with France was quickly made, though France still seemed the most likely of potential enemies. In 1560 Mary's husband Francis II became King of France; in Catholic eyes he had also a claim to be King of England but this danger vanished when Francis died. Moreover Mary, who had gone to rule Scotland, was eventually ousted by the Scottish Protestants, and forced into exile in England, where she virtually became Elizabeth's prisoner. Meanwhile, France settled down to a generation of strife between Catholic and Protestant, which at times almost eliminated her as an important factor in international politics.

But while France had been strong the countries which had most to fear from her, Spain and England, had been natural

allies. In the opening years of Elizabeth's reign this alliance was maintained. Philip made a half-hearted proposal of marriage to which Elizabeth gave a whole-hearted refusal. Yet it was largely because Philip acted as her protector that Elizabeth avoided excommunication from Rome until 1570. By the time the Bull of Excommunication came, it was not France, but Spain which loomed as the greatest threat to England's peace, if not her survival, and the main reason was the relentless policy of conformity which Philip was pursuing in the Netherlands.

In the Netherlands the seed of Protestantism, planted in the early years of the Reformation, had grown in the cosmopolitan atmosphere of Antwerp, and the other thriving towns which made the region the greatest commercial centre of the 16th century. Philip tried hard to crush the seed. In 1568 he sent an army under the Duke of Alva to stamp out Protestantism – and the political liberties demanded by Catholics and Protestants alike. But in Philip's lifetime there was to be no decision in the Netherlands. Year after year men and treasure were squandered in the campaign which, if often tantalizingly close to success, proved in the final analysis to be unwinnable. The result was a growing Protestant bastion which defied the might of Spain and which, before his death, Philip realized had frustrated his life's hopes. But it had been more than that. It was to play a fundamental role in bringing Philip to war against England.

The storm clouds gather

The prospect of a conflict with Spain was not one that Elizabeth and her more cautious Ministers would have welcomed, even if they had been confident of total victory. Indeed, the most important single thing to realize about the Anglo-Spanish conflict which led to the sailing of the Armada in 1588 is that it was not England's wish that the Spanish Empire should crumble. For if that happened there would be no obvious balance to the power of France, and it has always been self-evidently in England's interests that no one power should ever be in a position to dominate the Continent. What alarmed the English was that Philip's campaign to subdue Protestantism in the Netherlands meant the prospect of Spanish armies controlling the vital strategic area of the Low Countries. Elizabeth and her advisers were not prepared to see this happen. This preoccupation with the Netherlands has been a constant theme in English foreign policy right up to the 20th century. England has always been

17

The Escorial, Philip's gloomy monastery-palace, where he pondered on the affairs of his far-flung empire and the defiance of u heretic island to the north. Situated some 32 miles northwest of Madrid, the Escorial today contains one of the most valuable libraries of manuscripts and books in the world as well as a priceless collection of art treasures.

adamant that no great power dominates this area: in 1914 Britain went to war over Germany's violation of Belgian neutrality.

Elizabeth therefore sought to frustrate Philip's policy in the Netherlands. One way was by direct financial subsidies to the rebels. But there were other methods. In 1568 a fleet carrying an Italian loan to pay Spain's troops in the Netherlands sought refuge in an English harbour. Elizabeth simply took possession of the loan herself, which did not displease the Italians, who considered her much better security than Philip. Such acts were supplemented by attacks on Spanish shipping carried out in these years by famous 'sea dogs' whose exploits in the Spanish Main mark one of the high adventuring periods of English history. Men like Drake and Hawkins were no doubt as much pirates as anything else: but they were also anxious in England's interests to break the Spanish trading monopoly in the New World, and took a Protestant pride in their efforts. And, when successful, they met with the Queen's silent approval, particularly when she had herself a financial share in their activities.

The complex diplomacy in which Elizabeth was involved was to become still more tortuous when, in 1572, she expelled from England a group of nationalist Netherlands merchantmen. These men, known as the 'Sea Beggars', seized the Netherlands towns of Brill and Flushing and began a war of independence against Spain. Whether or not Elizabeth realized what they would do after she had expelled them is a matter for guesswork; but she may well have done. These Sea Beggars soon found a great leader in William the Silent, a member of the House of Orange, which was one day to provide an independent Holland with her rulers.

Elizabeth's policy in the 1570s and early 1580s was, then, to do all she could to hinder Philip in the Netherlands without committing herself to war on behalf of the rebels. Sometimes this meant close liaison with France which, though nominally under a Catholic king, had powerful Protestant and anti-Spanish factions who were willing to assist the enemies of Spain. The leader of this group was, by the late 1570s, the Duke of Alençon. An unprepossessing, pock-marked man, he yet enjoyed a remarkable personal as well as diplomatic flirtation with Elizabeth. When as a suitor for Elizabeth's hand he visited London in the summer of 1579, the Privy Councillors were positively horrified at the prospect of a French marriage; and at the affectionate way she fondled him in public and called him endearingly 'my frog'. Nevertheless, there was no marriage,

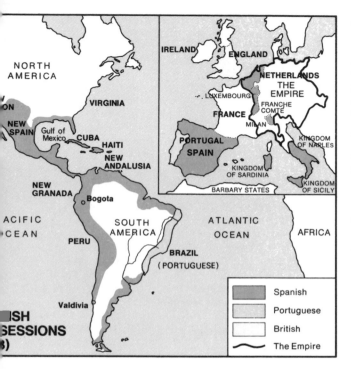

Europe and the New World, 1588. Spanish and Portuguese seamen, competing for a new route to the East Indies, carved out Catholic empires across the Atlantic. According to the terms of the Treaty of Tordesillas (1494), sanctioned by the Pope, Spain received the lion's share of the new discoveries, including islands in the West Indies and valuable territories in Central and South America. The Spanish possessions in the New World came to be known as the Spanish Main, and her galleons and colonies were systematically plundered by pirates and privateers of the Protestant maritime nations, led by such men as John Hawkins and his cousin Francis Drake.

and within a short time the personal element vanished, leaving a strictly business relationship.

For Philip, Elizabeth's policies were creating a situation he could not tolerate for long. Here was a sovereign, outlawed by the Church of which he was the leading temporal defender, giving aid to his greatest enemies at a point where he was deeply committed. He was maintaining a huge army in the Netherlands, which his nearly bankrupt country could ill-afford, but even this great military effort could not crush the defiant Dutch, staunchly defending their walled towns. Towards the end of the 1570s, a solution to his problems must have been taking shape in Philip's mind. Perhaps if the ally and subsidizer of the Dutch could be crushed, if Philip were to strike directly at England, then the situation in the Netherlands might be transformed. As Don John of Austria, one of Philip's commanders in the Netherlands, wrote to his sovereign: 'Everyone believes that the only remedy to the disorders of the Netherlands is for England to be ruled by some-one devoted to your Majesty. If the contrary case prevails it will mean the ruin of these countries and their loss to your Crown.'

But such a venture was still some way off. The relationship between Elizabeth and Philip in the 1570s and early 1580s degenerated into a 'cold war'. England, already threatened by the stream of Catholic missionaries landing in the country, was further alarmed by a series of Catholic plots in which the hand of Spain was very much apparent. In 1579 Catholic troops, in the name of the Papacy, tried unsuccessfully to raise Ireland against the Queen. In 1582 there was a Jesuit plot to raise Scotland. The focus of these plots was Mary Queen of Scots, whether they were conceived with or without her knowledge, for Catholic Mary would clearly have the best claim to the English throne if Elizabeth were disposed of. The Spanish Ambassadors in London played a leading part in fomenting these plots, and after one of them, in 1583, the Spanish ambassador Mendoza was expelled on the grounds that he had been disturbing the realm. His parting words were ominous: 'Bernadino di Mendoza was not born to disturb kingdoms but to conquer them.' He was the last Spanish Ambassador to the Queen's Court. Meanwhile, an even more menacing danger emerged as France plunged deeper into civil strife and Spain made an open bid to establish her own candidate, the Duke of Guise, on the French throne.

Not surprisingly the Elizabethan Government took action in the face of mounting tension. The legislation against Catholics

Robert Devereux, Earl of Essex was the last of Elizabeth's favourite courtiers. An impulsive, hot-tempered soldier, he was unsuccessful in quelling Tyrone's Irish rebellion and having lost the Queen's favours rashly tried to restore his position by force. He was tried for treason and executed in 1601.

moved from leniency to ferocity. Soon any missionary priest was *ipso facto* a traitor and many suffered the gruesome hanging, drawing, and quartering, which was the penalty for high treason.

In 1584 two events occurred which upset the delicate balance of the 'cold war'. Alençon died, which cut off French aid to the Dutch rebels, and William the Silent was assassinated by a fanatic, which raised the immediate prospect of Spanish victory in the Netherlands. Elizabeth had now to decide whether to give more substantial help to the rebels or watch them crushed.

This was a tense and fearful moment for her Government. England's security was jeopardized both by the Spanish advance in the Netherlands and by the mounting danger of a successful plot to end the Queen's life. Nothing perhaps illustrated quite so well the heightened emotions and mood of crisis than a remarkable document known as the 'Bond of Association'. This was a secret pledge drawn up by Elizabeth's Ministers which bound them on oath to destroy Mary Queen of Scots and bar her descendants from the English throne in the event of a successful plot in her name to eliminate Elizabeth – *even if Mary were ignorant of such a plot*. The Bond was circulated in the countryside in the autumn of 1584 and thousands of signatures were added.

But the crucial decision in the Netherlands remained to be taken. With reluctance, Elizabeth realized that she must make open war on Spain, and face the prospect of massive retaliation. It was a painful moment. For years both Elizabeth and Philip had endeavoured to preserve a fast-disappearing peace. Now events had moved out of the control of both of them. For Philip had determined that if he were to succeed in the Netherlands, England herself had to be crushed.

His decision was hardened by a further event. One Anthony Babington had plotted to restore Catholicism in England with Mary at its head. Mary, reckless as ever, committed her approval in writing. But the correspondence was all the time being read by Sir Francis Walsingham, at the head of the Elizabethan spy network. The evidence was overwhelming. On 18 February 1587 Mary was executed. All Catholic Europe looked to Philip to avenge it.

On 31 March 1587 Philip sent out a stream of letters from his lonely Escorial. They all breathed urgency. One of them, to his Captain-General for Ocean Seas, demanded that the invasion of England should be under way by the end of the coming spring.

The 'Enterprise of England'

By the end of May 1588, the Spanish Armada, the greatest concentration of naval might yet witnessed in Europe, had set sail on the 'Enterprise of England'. 'The Prudent King' was staking the whole prosperity of the Spanish Empire in this attempt to destroy the Protestant champion, the woman to whom he had once proposed marriage.

Left: *The Duke of Medina Sidonia, commander of the Armada – devout enough to be acceptable to God and noble enough to be acceptable to his subordinates.* **Right:** *Scourge of the Spanish Main, Sir Francis Drake. Prior to 'singeing the King of Spain's beard' Drake had sailed round the world, earning a knighthood in the teeth of Spanish protests.*

Philip's decision to launch the 'Enterprise of England' was not a sudden one, and it would have been quite uncharacteristic of the man called the 'Prudent King' if it had been. Some years before, his greatest admiral, Don Alvaro de Bazán, Marquis of Santa Cruz, had placed before him a plan for transporting the entire invasion force direct to England from Spain. Santa Cruz did not underestimate the task. The fleet he wanted would consist of over 500 ships, 150 of them either galleons or 'greatships'. He also wanted 40 galleys and 6 galleasses, with a total force of 30,000 mariners and 64,000 soldiers.

Galleons were the battleships of the 16th century. They were designed specifically for war, and were longer in proportion to their beams than the 'greatships', or armed merchantmen, which were primarily intended for commerce. Galleons usually had two or three decks and carried three masts. Most of them had elaborate 'castles' bristling with guns, built in the bow and stern, an outdated reminder of the days when sea fighting was thought of mainly as an extension of warfare on land. Their normal tactic was to close on the enemy and kill as many on the deck as possible with short-range 'man-killing' guns. Then they would move alongside and the real heroes, the soldiers, would board the enemy ship and complete the victory. The Spaniards clung to these old-fashioned ideas longer than the English.

Galleys had quite a different purpose. They were low, narrow, sleek vessels propelled by the oars of the galley-slaves. They were therefore extremely manoeuvrable, and their sharp bows were intended to ram enemy ships and disable them. It was largely by using his galleys that Santa Cruz had won his renowned victory over the Turks at Lepanto, in 1571; one of the most critical

battles of the Western world, since it stemmed the tide of the Turkish advance into Europe. But galleys could not be nearly as formidable in the heavy waters of the Atlantic, nor could they be as effective against the vast warships of the Elizabethan navy, which they could scarcely hope to get near, let alone damage by ramming. Therefore, the Spanish developed another type of ship, the galleass. It had sail and oar, was heavier than a galley but lighter than a galleon, and was supposed to combine the virtues of both.

Santa Cruz's estimate may well have been reasonable considering the task ahead, but it was far beyond the resources of a Spanish King who was always hovering on the verge of bankruptcy. However, there was an alternative plan, put forward by Alexander Farnese, Duke of Parma, commander of Philip's troops in the Netherlands and acknowledged to be the finest military leader of his age. Parma had devoted his life to reconquering the Netherlands for Spain, and was as concerned as anybody that English assistance to the rebels should be stopped. He had the most experienced and consistently successful troops in Europe at his disposal, just across the Channel from the English coast. If 30,000 infantry and 4,000 cavalry could be assembled at the right place at the right time, they could embark in flat-bottomed boats, make the crossing in a single night, and defeat the English without bringing Elizabeth's formidable navy into the struggle at all.

Such was Parma's plan, and it presented some terrifying dangers for Spain. In the first place, 30,000 troops could hardly subdue the entire nation, unless, as Parma anticipated, there was a spontaneous rising of England's Catholics against the heretic Queen. There is something pathetic in the often-repeated assurances, estimates, and predictions by kings, popes, and English Catholic exiles that one-third or more of the English people were ready to fly to arms in the Catholic cause as soon as an invasion was attempted. They could not have been more wrong. When the invasion came there was not a single instance of English Catholics rising against their Protestant Queen.

Parma's plan had a second danger: his army might be isolated in England, with his supplies and lines of communication cut off by the English navy. Furthermore, unless the English navy was caught completely unawares, Parma's army would be sent to the bottom of the sea before it had an opportunity to fight at all. Philip himself realized the difficulty, and alongside Parma's

comment that absolute secrecy was vital, the King perceptively wrote 'hardly possible'.

Although both schemes presented to Philip – those of Santa Cruz and Parma – were out of the question, Philip derived from them a plan of his own. He would indeed prepare a mighty armada, but it would not be as mighty as Santa Cruz had wanted, nor would so much be expected from it. It would not itself carry the invading army. Instead, it would sail up the Channel, rendezvous with Parma's barges off the Low Countries, and escort them in safety to the English coast. Thus the Armada simply had to be strong enough to win command of the Channel.

But this was an extremely formidable task. Despite a certain amount of activity, the Spanish fleet was in little more than skeleton form when, on 31 March 1587, Philip sent his decisive message to Santa Cruz that all haste should be made and that the fleet should sail before the summer.

The dragon strikes

In London, Elizabeth could not know that the die was now cast. She still hoped that open war with Spain could be avoided, and she was actually negotiating with Parma for a settlement which could bring peace to the Netherlands at the very moment the Spanish invasion fleet was being mounted.

Such an attitude baffled her staunch Protestant subjects, some of whom sat in her Privy Council, some in the House of Commons, and others of whom sailed the high seas in search of Spanish gold. Sir Francis Walsingham, the Queen's Secretary of State, could make no sense of it at all; nor could the vociferous Puritans, who put forward demands in the Commons in 1586–7 that Elizabeth's subsidy be made conditional on her accepting the sovereignty of the Netherlands, in open defiance of Spain. And particularly exasperated was a man who had long considered himself at war with the King of Spain, whatever the Queen's feelings on the subject might be: Sir Francis Drake. Some twenty years earlier, at San Juan de Ulua, young Francis Drake had been one of the few survivors of a trading mission which had been attacked and destroyed by the Spaniards. Since then he had pursued a career of revenge which made his very name an object of terror on Spanish coastlines, in Europe and the New World. To the Spaniards he was 'El Draque' (the Dragon); many believed he had a magic mirror which told him the whereabouts of Spanish treasure ships, because he located and plundered them

A contemporary print of Cadiz, where Drake 'singed the King of Spain's beard' in the spring of 1587, delaying the sailing of the Armada for more than a year.

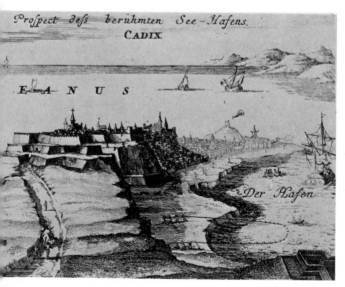

27

The Spaniards sent 130 vessels to sea, of which twenty were galleons such as these, armed with heavy 50-pounder cannons. They were outfought and out-manoevred by the lighter and more mobile English warships, especially at close quarters.

unerringly. From the King downwards Spaniards spoke of Drake and the English navy as synonymous.

Drake's response to the Spanish preparation was simple: he would cripple them in their own harbours before they could get to sea. But he had to wait for permission from the Queen, and this, it seemed, would never come. Finally, the rumour that the Spaniards would come in spring forced a decision from the reluctant Queen: Drake got his instructions on 25 March, and they were all he could have wished for. He was to 'impeach the purpose of the Spanish fleet and stop them meeting in Lisbon' (the rendezvous for the Spanish fleet), even if it meant 'distressing their ships within their havens'. But the Queen gave Drake more than these orders. She also contributed 6 ships, including 4 galleons, one of which was the 550-ton flagship, *Elizabeth Bonaventure*. With these, 4 of his own ships, a contribution from the Admiral of the Fleet, Lord Howard, and others to bring his total strength to over 20 ships, Drake hurried away just in time to miss a message from the Queen changing her instructions: 'You shall forbear', she said, 'to enter forcibly into any of the said King's ports or havens, or to offer violence to any of his towns or shipping within harbouring, or to do any act of hostility upon the land.'

Had this message been received, it would have prevented an exploit immortalized in Drake's own phrase as the 'singeing of the King of Spain's beard'. At four o'clock on the afternoon of Wednesday, 24 April, the peace of Cadiz harbour was shattered by the appearance of Drake's fleet sweeping irresistibly into the harbour itself. Throughout that evening, all night, and the following day, the English played havoc with the ships at Cadiz. According to Drake he destroyed thirty-seven of them, according to the Spaniards twenty-four. Among them were a 700-ton Genoese merchantman, sent to the bottom with her forty brass cannon, and a great galleon belonging to Santa Cruz himself. Many of the ships must have been intended to join Santa Cruz at Lisbon, and indeeed the raid on Cadiz virtually wiped out one section of the Armada. But Drake was not finished. He made for Cape St Vincent, took possession of it, and intercepted cargoes of hoops and barrel-staves bound for Lisbon. These may not sound glamorous prizes, but fresh barrel-staves were essential for the preservation of food and drink on a major expedition. Drake's barrel-staves were to cast a long shadow over the Armada.

Before he returned home Drake had another success: he

captured the Portuguese *San Felipe*, one of the richest prizes ever taken, worth £114,000. Drake had not only 'impeached the purpose of the Spanish fleet' but he had also shown a handsome profit, of which the Queen's share was £40,000.

Drake returned home in mid June, knowing that while he had delayed the Spaniards, he had certainly not prevented the invasion altogether. While off Cape St Vincent he had written to Walsingham, 'I assure your Honour, the like preparation was never heard of or known as the King of Spain hath and daily maketh to invade England. . . . This service which by God's sufferance we have done will breed some alteration of their pretences: nevertheless, all possible preparations for defence are very expedient to be made.'

He was right. Philip's hopes of getting the Armada to sea by the summer were abandoned, but he gave fresh orders to Santa Cruz to sail in September. Philip acted like a man transformed. No longer the 'Prudent King', he had become almost fanatical in his haste to set the Armada afloat. Again and again Santa Cruz begged for delay. Their ships had not all assembled; their guns were inadequate; there were insufficient provisions. Grudgingly, the King granted a series of postponements, usually of a few weeks. But he was determined that in December the Armada should sail, even if only thirty-odd ships were ready, and even if Santa Cruz did not go himself. This instruction brought a flurry of answering activity in England, where the Queen's navy was on full alert within a fortnight, an indication of the difficulty the Spaniards had in keeping their plans secret. But the immediate crisis passed. Santa Cruz won further delays, and then, early in February, when he had finally decided to put to sea come what may, he fell ill and took to his bed. On the ninth of the month the great naval hero died.

Santa Cruz was one of the most famous sailors of his day: his spectacular victories over the Turks and Portuguese had already passed into legend. But his successor, Alonso Perez de Guzmán el Bueno, Duke of Medina Sidonia, enjoyed no such reputation, and he for one thought himself a very bad choice. He wrote: 'I know by experience of the little I have been at sea that I am always seasick and always catch cold.' And 'since I have had no experience either of the sea or of war, I cannot feel that I ought to command so important an enterprise'. But he was overruled. The King wanted nothing now but for the Armada to be under way, and Medina Sidonia was devout enough to be acceptable

Philip II of Spain. No longer the 'Prudent King', he had become almost fanatical in his haste to launch the Armada against England. His plans, based on wishful thinking and poor intelligence, were doomed from the start. Philip accepted the Armada's defeat philosophically, ascribing it to storms rather than English superiority.

to God and noble enough to be acceptable to his subordinates.

Up to a point, Medina Sidonia proved remarkably more suitable than his own estimate would suggest. For one thing he was certainly prepared to listen to advice, and he immediately set up a kind of War Council of three of his ablest commanders, the experienced Pedro de Valdes, the dashing Miguel de Oquendo, and Juan Martinez de Recalde, second only in fame to Santa Cruz himself. With the help of these, Medina Sidonia set about rectifying the mess he found waiting for him at Lisbon. Some ships there had no guns or provisions, while others were practically sinking through overloading. Many of the crews were badly clothed and diseased. Preparations had been under way for so long that high mortality and desertion rates were inevitable. Above all, there were not enough powerful ships equipped with long-range guns.

The Armada prepares

Over the next three months Medina Sidonia did much to remedy these defects. He saw to it that more guns, though still not enough, were cast or unearthed; supplies were redistributed, and the large ships gained at the expense of the smaller ones. The amount of gunpowder was doubled, and the rounds of the great guns were increased from thirty to fifty. But he could do little about the foul state of provisions and drinking-water, and this problem worsened every day. Nevertheless, by late April, when eight splendid galleons from Portugal had joined the fleet, an armada had assembled which looked formidable by any standards.

The first line of battle was under the command of Medina Sidonia in the *San Martin*, advised by his Chief of Staff, Diego de Flores. It consisted of 10 galleons from the Portuguese Navy (including the Florentine *Florencia* appropriated for the occasion), 10 galleons from Castile, 4 greatships, and 4 galleasses. The second line was composed of 40 greatships divided into 4 squadrons named after the regions from which they came. The Biscayans were under Recalde in the *San Juan*; the Guipuzcoans were led by Oquendo, the Andalusians by Pedro de Valdes, and the Levanters by Martin de Bertendona. Bertendona's squadron carried the commander of the land forces, the dashing de Leyva, in the *Rata Coronada*. Apart from the main fighting vessels, there were store-ships, transports, scouting-ships, and messengers. In all, there were 130 ships, 10,000 sailors, and 19,000 soldiers. It is an interesting commentary on Spanish priorities that there were

150 gunners and 180 priests.

All the details – numbers of men, guns, quantity of powder and stores – were noted down and published as an official document. Soon the list, or versions of it, was being read all over Europe. Protestant printers often added such instruments of torture as seemed to them to suit the requirements of their readers. But in any case, the strength of the Armada was to be no secret – it was a propaganda weapon intended to overawe its enemies before the fleet even entered the arena.

On 25 April, the Duke of Medina Sidonia received the blessing of the Archbishop of Lisbon, at the Cathedral, and was presented with a standard bearing the inscription: 'Arise, O Lord, and Vindicate Thy Cause.' All the soldiers and sailors confessed, were absolved, and received the blessing. A fortnight later the Armada was ordered to sail, and though bad weather caused long delays, by 30 May the entire fleet was at sea, and the 'Enterprise of England' was on its way.

Everyone in Spain seems to have been confident. The King and even Medina Sidonia certainly were. But there may have been some on board the Spanish ships who recalled that the astrologers and fortune-tellers had long been prophesying disasters on a cataclysmic scale for the year 1588 when, 'will the whole world suffer upheavals, empires will dwindle, and from everywhere will be great lamentations'.

The Battle of England

Beacons flared across England when the Armada was sighted. Along the south coast the battle thundered. Over 200 ships were involved. But when the Armada anchored off Calais, though badly mauled, it was still a powerfull force, still capable of escorting Parma's troops across the Channel. The battle of England was by no means over.

In the foreground is a Spanish galleon, behind it the more efficient galleass. Both sailed against the English fleet and met a similar fate.

According to the famous story, on the afternoon of Friday, 29 July 1588, Sir Francis Drake was playing bowls on Plymouth Hoe. Suddenly, Captain Fleming, from one of the scouting vessels, came running up to him, breathless and agitated. The Armada had been sighted off the Lizard! Sir Francis replied, 'We have time enough to finish the game and beat the Spaniards too'; then he turned his attention back to the green.

Drake, if he said the words attributed to him, was indeed astonishingly cool. For he knew well that the south-west wind bringing the Armada towards Plymouth was blowing straight into the Sound and would seriously handicap the efforts of the English fleet to leave the port and reach the open sea.

Yet England's seamen had many good reasons to be confident. Although about half their fleet was many miles away, guarding the narrow seas against the Duke of Parma, the ships in Plymouth included eighteen great galleons, many of them new or streamlined along the lines laid down by Sir John Hawkins, the head of the Admiralty. The English were relying on speed, manœuvrability, and the power of long-range guns, techniques quite unlike those of the Spaniards, who preferred to come to close range and board the enemy with overwhelming numbers of soldiers. Above all, the English had their sailors – more than the Spaniards – though they carried only one-tenth the number of soldiers brought by the Armada. Among England's seamen were some of the greatest captains of the age, Drake himself, John Hawkins, and Martin Frobisher. The Lord Admiral was Lord Howard of Effingham, who, if inexperienced, at least had a great love of the sea and knew how to take advice.

In short, the years before the Armada had seen the English

A set of contemporary maps, showing the running battle which took place between the English fleet and the Armada along the south coast of England. **1** *The English fleet massing in Plymouth Sound to meet the Spanish threat.* **2** *The Spanish Armada off the Lizard.*

fleet develop into a formidable, but untested, weapon. And the hours following Fleming's message were spent ensuring that that weapon was not caught in Plymouth and smashed before it had a chance to show what it could do. The preparations went on at a frantic pace. Additional stores were taken on board at the last minute, numerous rowing-boats towed the large warships to the mouth of the Sound where they could catch the wind and tack their way out to sea. As darkness fell the first of the great English warships left the Sound ready to do battle for England.

There was far less urgency among the Spaniards than among the English. The Duke of Medina Sidonia was in no mood to

1

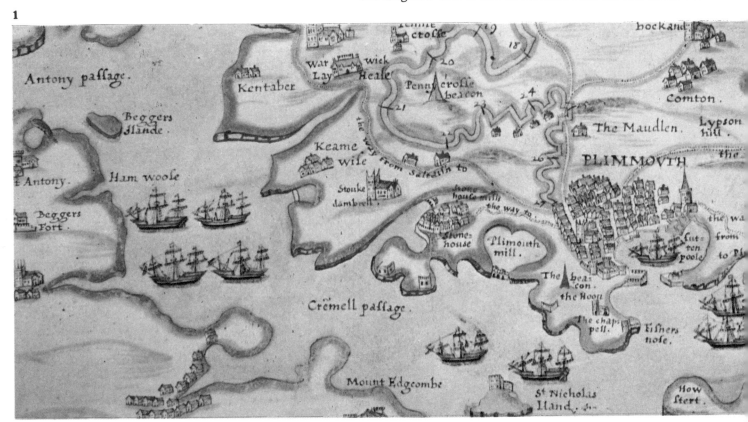

run any risks – he was thankful enough to have retained all but a handful of his original Armada following unseasonably rough weather on the journey from Lisbon. A dash to Plymouth to catch the English with their backs to the coast would have meant splitting the Armada which naturally moved at the pace of its slowest hulks. In any case, his orders from the King were to use the Armada to ferry the Duke of Parma's troops across to England and he had no intention of disobeying his instructions.

And so, without worrying unduly, the Spaniards drifted slowly half-way between the Lizard and Plymouth on the night of 29 July. Their vast fleet, 'beneath the weight of which the

2

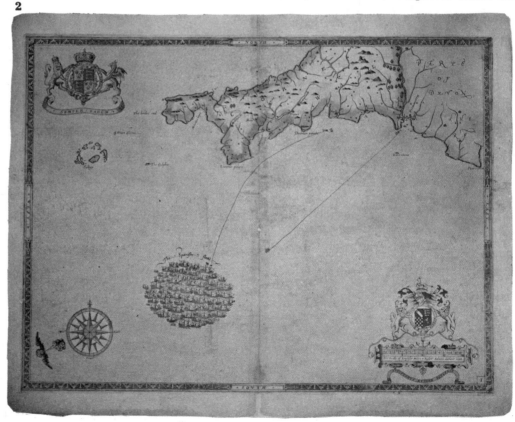

The two fleets clash. **3** *The Armada forms the famous crescent to protect itself against the attacks of the English fleet emerging from Plymouth.* **4** *The Armada sails on, harried continually by the English ships, until it reaches Portland Bill (at right of picture) where a general engagement takes place.* **5** *After the battle off Portland the Armada re-forms, and sets its course towards the Isle of Wight where the Spaniards had originally intended to land, but the English fleet, forming four blocks, forces it out to sea and on to Calais.*

sea seemed to groan', was spread over several miles of sea: a menacing, awesome spectacle to those who watched apprehensively from the coast. Already England's alert was on. Warning beacons flashed news of the Spaniards' arrival along the coast and inland to every county. The Duke wrote: 'The Armada was very near the shore. We were seen by the people on land, who made fires and smokes.' It must have been as eerie for the Spaniards as for the English, peering in the fading light at their respective enemies, wondering what the following days had in store. The last thing Medina Sidonia saw before darkness was a group of English ships to leeward. It was a comforting sight. The

3

4

English were between the Armada and the shore and he had no doubt that they would be there the next day.

But dawn brought a nasty shock. The ships he had seen the previous night had been the stragglers who had not got out of Plymouth with the main body of the fleet. This main body – fifty-four sail – now appeared in the rear of the Armada, bearing down with the same south-west wind that had given the Spaniards their own cause for optimism. Seeing the danger, Medina Sidonia in the *San Martin* signalled, and the whole fleet re-organized its formation with extraordinary precision, to confront the new danger. The new formation was the famous crescent, or

5

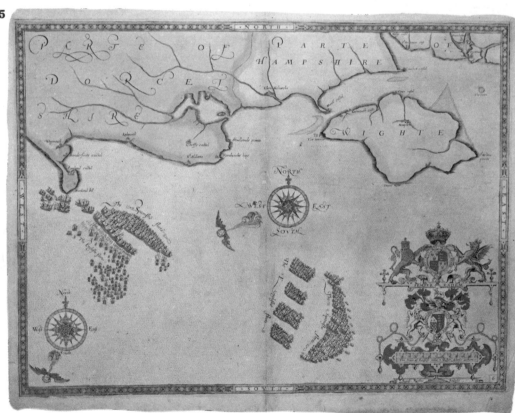

half-moon, commented on so frequently by English observers. At the centre were the galleons of Portugal and Castile headed by Medina Sidonia. In an arc the four squadrons – Recalde and his Biscayans on the extreme left, followed by the Andalusians; and on the right the Guipuzcoans and the Levanters. Clustered in the middle, sheltered by the 'Main Battle' in the centre, came the defenceless store-ships and hulks.

The fleets clash

The proceedings opened with a small ceremony in which Howard formally delivered his defiance. He sent a tiny pinnace, appropriately called the *Disdain*, right out ahead of the fleet whereupon it fired one of its popguns.

Then the English fleet, the wind behind it, sailed across the Armada crescent from the right. Howard, in the *Ark Royal*, exchanged fire with Bertendona, and much of the Armada's right wing, in confusion, pressed dangerously towards the centre. Desperately, de Leyva, in the *Rata Coronada* and Oquendo's flagship tried to rally the fast-dissolving right, but meanwhile other English ships, including Drake's *Revenge*, Hawkins's *Victory*, and Frobisher's *Triumph*, crossed over to the left wing where a fierce battle developed around Recalde in the *San Juan*. Recalde lost contact with the rest of the Armada and was pounded at long range by the English. It seems unlikely that so experienced a sailor could have found himself in such a position by mistake. Possibly he was trying to tempt the English to try a boarding, whereupon the rest of the Armada might return for a general mêlée which he knew to be the Spaniards' best chance of victory. But the English, if they were tempted, did not respond and eventually the rest of the Biscayan squadron 'rescued' Recalde and escorted him back to the main body of the Armada.

This opening encounter was an unnerving experience for the Spaniards who, for the first time, saw to what an extent their slow-moving vessels were outclassed by the English. Medina Sidonia wrote in bewilderment of 'their ships being very nimble and of such good steerage as they did with them whatsoever they desired'. Confronted by such a foe, the Spaniards had already showed signs of panic, suffered considerable damage and casualties, and yet had not managed to do any of the English ships the slightest harm. Above all, it was clear that the English were all able to stand off and pound the Armada from a distance and that they could not be manœuvred into the close-range, quarter-

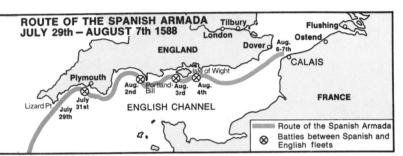

The progress of the Spanish Armada towards Calais. Three major actions were fought – off Plymouth, Portland Bill and the Isle of Wight. None were decisive, for the English guns were not powerful enough to penetrate the hulls of the galleons and armed merchantmen at long range.

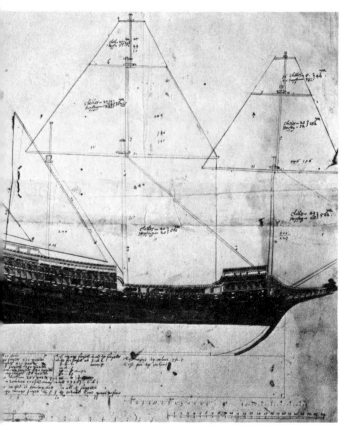

Plan of an English galleon. It was faster and more manoeuvrable than its unwieldy Spanish counterpart and its guns were of lighter weight and had a longer range. In the final stages of the encounter the English broadsides, fired at point-blank range, had a devastating effect.

deck to quarter-deck confrontation, on which the Spaniards, with their thousands of otherwise useless soldiers, depended. Clearly, the Armada was in for a testing time, and just as clearly, discipline must be tightened to prevent a repetition of the chaos of the first battle. The Armada's War Diary recorded that the sergeant-majors were dispatched with orders, in writing: 'To immediately hang any Captain whose ship left her place, and they took with them the Provost-Marshals and Hangmen necessary for carrying out this order.'

Howard broke off the fighting about midday and the two fleets did little more than eye each other warily for the rest of the afternoon. But the peace of the afternoon was shattered when one of the Spanish flagships, the *San Salvador*, suddenly blew up (whether by accident or sabotage is unknown). Anxiously, Medina Sidonia set about taking off the wounded and arranging a tow for the burning ship. But before dark there was an even more alarming development. The *Rosario*, commanded by Don Pedro de Valdes, had collided with another ship during the re-formation of the Armada after the morning's engagement, and her bow had been seriously damaged. Now she began to flounder and fall behind. Medina Sidonia took the *San Martin* close, hoping to tow the stricken ship himself. A cable was passed, but in the rapidly rising seas it snapped. The Duke's chief adviser, Don Diego de Valdes, a kinsman of Don Pedro, but also his inveterate enemy, suggested that they abandon the *Rosario* lest the English catch up with the whole Armada during the night. Reluctantly the Duke accepted this advice.

On Sunday evening, 31 July, the English held a Council of War aboard the *Ark Royal*. They decided that their best policy was to follow the Armada up the Channel and only give battle at those points where it seemed that a possible landing might be made. One possibility was Portland Bill; by far the most likely, the Isle of Wight. The chase, or rather procession, was to begin that evening and Howard courteously allowed Drake to lead the pursuit. The lantern of the *Revenge* was to guide Howard and the rest of the fleet, but that night, for some reason, the watch on board the *Ark Royal* lost sight of Drake's lantern. After a little while a light appeared some distance away and, presuming it to be Drake, Howard with two other ships in attendance, hurried after it. At dawn the Lord Admiral was disconcerted to find that he had been following the light of an enemy ship and that he and his two companions were practically in the jaws of the Armada. We do

41

A souvenir print. The Armada, formed in its awesome defensive crescent, under attack by the English fleet.

not know exactly what happened next or how Howard extricated himself. It is conceivable that Medina Sidonia felt too chivalrous to take advantage of the Lord Admiral's plight. In any case Howard scurried back to rejoin the English fleet, no doubt intensely curious to find out where Drake had got to.

Drake, apparently by an extraordinary stroke of luck which made Martin Frobisher, for one, black with rage, had happened to stumble across the *Rosario*. It was the richest prize taken from the Armada. In addition to the ship itself, its guns and equipment, Drake took possession of the treasure chest of 55,000 ducats and, typically, took Pedro de Valdes aboard as an honoured guest to witness the battle from the other side.

The fiery Frobisher's report some weeks later was:
'Sir Francis Drake reporteth that no man hath done any good service but he; but he shall understand that others hath done as good service as he, and better too. He hath done good service indeed, for he took Don Pedro. For after he had seen her [the *Rosario*] in the evening, that she had spent her masts, then like a coward, he kept by her all night, because he would have the spoil. He thinketh to cozen us of our shares of 15,000 ducats; but we will have our shares, or I will make him spend the best blood in his belly; for we hath had enough of those cozening cheats already.'

Later on that day, the English picked up the burnt-out wreck of the *San Salvador*; the men had been taken off, but a fair quantity of powder and ammunition remained which the English gratefully seized to supplement their dwindling supplies.

Portland Bill and the Isle of Wight

On the night of 2 August, both fleets anchored off Portland Bill, one of those potential landing-places the English were determined to defend. But the morning found the Spaniards in a position to take the offensive, for the wind was blowing off the land, from the north-east, and the Spaniards were able to bear down on the English. Howard tried to edge along the coast round the left of the Armada, but found himself unable to do so.

He then moved across the crescent and, in conjunction with Hawkins, began a fierce engagement with Bertendona's squadron on the right. It must have been a thrilling sight. The great English warships, *Ark Royal*, *Golden Lion*, *White Bear*, *Elizabeth Jonas*, *Victory*, *Nonpareil*, were challenging *Reganzona*, *San Marcos*, *San Luis*, *San Mateo*, *Rata Coronada*, *Santa Anna*, *San*

Felipe. The thunder of guns echoed across miles of sea and could be clearly heard on land. Meanwhile, Martin Frobisher in the *Triumph* remained on the left and it looked as though he had got himself into an impossible position. Apparently pinned back against the coast, the *Triumph* was engaged in a furious bombardment with the four galleasses under Hugh de Moncada in the *San Lorenzo*. The fight was, as Hawkins described it, 'sharp and long', but up to this point one great seaman had played no part. Under cover of the billowing clouds of smoke, Drake and some fifty ships had made their way out to sea on the land breeze. Suddenly the wind changed, blowing strongly from the southwest, bringing Drake sweeping down on the right wing of the Armada, with the wind straight behind him.

The galleasses were withdrawn from their duel with Frobisher to meet the new danger, and Recalde – in the thick of the fighting as usual – had to be relieved by a detachment of Spanish galleons. At one point, Medina Sidonia thought he could bring about a personal confrontation with his opposite number in the *Ark Royal*. He struck his topsails in preparation for grappling and boarding, but Lord Howard responded by leading his ships one by one past the *San Martin*, each giving her a broadside as they did so. As the Duke put it: 'When my flagship saw that the flagship of the enemy was heading towards her, she lowered her topsails, but the enemy's flagship passed her, followed by the whole of his Fleet and shot at her, ship by ship, as it passed.' This was not the kind of warfare the Duke had expected. For nearly an hour the *San Martin* withstood the onslaught alone, replying as best she could, before Oquendo came up with a relief force and the English retired.

There was little fighting on 3 August. For one thing, both sides were seriously short of ammunition and Lord Howard sent ashore for further supplies. He also took the opportunity to reorganize his fleet into four squadrons, under himself, Drake, Hawkins, and Frobisher. The only serious incident of the day occurred when the giant Spanish galleon *Gran Grifon* dropped behind the rest of the fleet and was pounded by Drake. Her casualties numbered seventy dead and seventy wounded before Recalde's squadron came to the rescue.

The following day, 4 August, saw both fleets off the Isle of Wight. This was a critical moment. The English considered this by far the likeliest place for a landing: indeed, a few days previously the Duke had written to the King: 'The object of the

Charles, Lord Howard of Effingham, Lord Admiral of England. Although relatively inexperienced, he was prepared to accept the advice of younger men. He enjoyed the solid support of such seasoned campaigners as John Hawkins and Martin Frobisher (both of whom he knighted after the battle off the Isle of Wight) and the redoutable Sir Francis Drake.

present letter is to say that I am obliged to proceed slowly with all the Armada together in squadrons as far as the Isle of Wight, and no further.'

But there was no wind at all that morning and in order to prevent the Spaniards from landing the English had to bring about a battle. Desperately, Hawkins had his *Victory* towed by rowing-boats into the range of a couple of Spanish stragglers. Medina Sidonia sent out his galleasses to confront Hawkins. This was ideal weather for the galleasses, and after a fierce exchange, they were able to return to the fleet together with the stragglers. Meanwhile, an action had developed that was almost an exact repetition of the Battle of Portland Bill. Once again Frobisher found himself with his back to the coast, an easy prey to the Spaniards. And again the wind changed to the south-west, enabling Frobisher to sail rapidly away from the incoming Spaniards. And this south-west wind also brought Drake, this time accompanied by Hawkins, sweeping in from the far right. The right of the Spanish crescent was in danger of total disintegration. The Spaniards fell back close to the coast and were shepherded along by the pursuing English. Suddenly, Medina Sidonia realized that in front of him was not deep water but the jutting reefs and crags of the dangerous Ower Bank. Seeing the peril, he fired a warning shot and set out into deeper water, followed by the rest of the Armada.

The English had most certainly won a tactical victory. They had not broken the Armada, but then they had not seriously tried to do so. What they had done was to prevent any possibility of the Spaniards landing in the most favourable places. In some ways, it might have seemed that the English had exceptional luck in these battles, the winds shifting suddenly in their favour. But in fact this was not the case. The summer wind in the Channel usually blows off shore in the early part of the morning, followed later by the normal south-westerly. There is no reason to believe that Drake was not aware of this when in both battles he sailed seaward on the land breeze, to return like an avenging angel on the south-westerly. Nor need we believe that Frobisher was not in complete control of his own situation. At both Portland Bill and the Isle of Wight there are strong tidal currents running within a few yards of each other. To anyone who knew the waters as Frobisher did, the business of moving from one current to another, to slide easily out of the range of the Spanish ships was no great problem, and one which did not depend solely on the wind.

45

The Ark Royal, the Lord Admiral's flagship. He considered her sailing qualities to be unrivalled. Rumours that she had been captured were unfounded and the ship performed with distinction throughout the engagement with the Armada.

The Spaniards were far less happy. They had now entered the most difficult part of the Channel without finding a landing-place, and their food and water were by now putrid. They had no prospect of supplies of desperately needed powder and ammunition. Above all, they had heard nothing from the Duke of Parma. Medina Sidonia sent long streams of messages imploring him to send supplies or to send ships or to embark his troops immediately. Something had to be done quickly. Already the Armada was beginning to suffer from the attacks of the English fleet. On the afternoon of 6 August the Armada anchored off Calais, hoping that news from Parma would not be long delayed.

That evening the English fleet was joined by thirty-five ships, including five royal galleons under Lord Henry Seymour. These ships had been blockading the Netherlands coast in case Parma should come out. This duty was now eagerly taken over by a Dutch fleet.

So the English fleet had gained in strength considerably since those fifty-four ships had left the Sound in search of the Armada. There were now over 140 – a numerical superiority for the first time. On Sunday, 7 August, Lord Howard called another conference aboard the *Ark Royal*. The English now decided that the one way to disperse the great defensive crescent of the Armada was to set a number of ships on fire and sail them down-wind into the heart of the Spanish fleet. This decision was to prove decisive in the story of the Spanish Armada.

Victory for England

Eight small, blazing ships put the Armade to rout. Crippled, it limped away to begin the terrible voyage home around the top of Scotland. Storms, cold, hunger, shipwreck, and the wild Irish beset the once mighty fleet. Defeat was turned into disaster.

A large warship of the late 16th century clearly showing the sail plan. Particularly noticeable was the exaggerated high aft and long forward beak.

Sunday 6 August was an uneasy day for the Spaniards, anchored just two miles off Calais, in sight of the English fleet. For one thing, they had had no satisfactory news from the Duke of Parma who was supposed to be ready to come out with his troops at any moment. In fact, Parma had no intention of risking his superb soldiers in their flimsy open boats against both the English navy and the hungry Dutch fleet under Justin of Nassau. As Parma wrote to Philip:

'To judge from what the Duke [Medina Sidonia] says, it would appear that he still expects me to come out to join him with our boats, although it must be perfectly clear that this is not feasible. Most of our boats are built only for the rivers, and they are unable to weather the least sea. It is quite as much as they can do to carry over the men in perfectly fair weather, but as for fighting as well, it is evident they cannot do it, however good the troops in them may be.'

But the Armada – which was supposed to win command of the Channel and so make any sea-fighting on Parma's part unnecessary – had so far proved unable seriously to damage a single English ship. Moreover, Spanish supplies and ammunition had run critically low, and they got little comfort from the Governor of Calais, Monsieur Gourdan, who, together with his wife, had installed himself by the shore ready to watch the imminent battle. Monsieur Gourdan merely warned the Spaniards that the Channel currents made their anchorage particularly dangerous and sent a small basket of fruit for Medina Sidonia's personal consumption.

But the thing that most worried the Spaniards was the ceaseless to-ing and fro-ing among the English fleet as it was being

Left: A model showing the attack of the fire-ships, with the English ships in the background, ready to move in. Panic broke out in the Spanish fleet as the fire-ships approached, for they were believed to be replicas of the explosive-laden 'hell-burners' employed by the Dutch at Antwerp. Cables were cut and ships collided with one another in their eagerness to escape the flames.
Following pages: The dreaded fire-ships attack the great Armada. Its formation is broken and it prepares to flee. The chaos caused by the fire-ships culminated in the crucial battle off Gravelines.

reinforced by the Channel squadrons of Seymour and Wynter. For the Spaniards were convinced that the English were up to some diabolical plan. Long ago Philip had warned Medina Sidonia to expect the English to use 'strange fireworks', and many Spaniards remembered the terrible 'hell burners' used against them by the Dutch in the siege of Antwerp three years earlier. 'Hell burners' were no ordinary fire-ships but, rather, floating bombs packed with high explosive and slow-burning fuses, which within moments could kill a thousand men. Spanish fears were increased by the knowledge that the Italian inventor of these 'hell burners', Giambelli, was in England at the time. No wonder one Spanish officer wrote of: 'a great presentiment of evil from that devilish people and their arts [as] in a great watching we continued on Sunday all day long'.

In fact, Giambelli was not occupied in anything devilish but was employed in constructing a harmless boom across the Thames. The fire-ships that were being prepared by the English were simply normal tools of 16th-century naval warfare. There were eight of them altogether, including one each from the squadrons of Drake and Hawkins. They were stripped of their stores, but their guns were left double-loaded, to explode in the intense heat. Then, shortly before midnight on Sunday, they were lashed together, fired, and launched under full sail against the Spanish fleet.

The fire ships

Medina Sidonia had anticipated the use of fire-ships and arranged for a screen of pinnaces to go out and meet the line of blazing ships and, using grappling-irons, tow them inshore away from the Armada. It was a tricky and dangerous operation, and the Spaniards watched anxiously as the tiny pinnaces confronted the wall of flame towering above them. They managed to haul away two of the fire-ships but then the double-loaded cannons began to explode, and in the pinnaces, and all over the Spanish fleet, there was sudden panic. The 'hell burners' had returned! Nobody in the Armada realized that these were ordinary fire-ships. But the damage was done. On a strong wind and a full current, the fire-ships swept past the disorganized pinnaces, and confusion reigned as the Spaniards cut their cables and ran before the wind, their great ships sometimes crashing into each other in their efforts to get away. Hugh de Moncada's galleass, *San Lorenzo*, was crippled in a collision and lost her

51

Right: *The decisive Battle of Gravelines – the moment the English fleet had been waiting for. The Spanish ships, fleeing in terror from the fire-ships, scattered in confusion – easy targets for the English fleet which came bearing down on them, sails billowing. Total destruction seemed inevitable.* **Below:** *Contemporary map shows the scattered remnants of the invincible Armada fleeing up the North Sea, chased by the victorious English fleet. There was nothing the Spaniards could do now to reverse the disastrous defeat. Their fleet was in a desperate plight: morale was low, and one-fifth of the men were dead or wounded.*

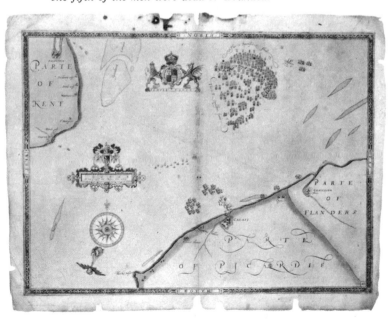

rudder. As dawn broke, the formidable formation which the Spaniards had maintained for so long had at last been broken. The only ships in view of the *San Martin* were Recalde's *San Juan*, two other Portuguese galleons, and the helpless *San Lorenzo*. In the words of one Spaniard, 'fortune so favoured the English that there grew from these pieces of industry just what they counted on, for they dislodged us with 8 vehicles, an exploit which with 130 they had not been able nor dared to attempt. When the morning came they had gained the weather gauge of us, for we found ourselves scattered in every direction.' This was the moment the English had been waiting for. From their fleet a gun boomed, and with sails billowing, the whole English fleet – the six squadrons of Howard, Drake, Hawkins, Frobisher, Seymour, and Wynter – bore down on the remnants of the invincible Armada.

Medina Sidonia had no intention of shirking his duty in that desperate moment. He stood out to sea, his handful of companions beside him, to take the full brunt of the English onslaught, and he dispatched small boats in all directions to round up the ships scattered in the night and to tell them to return once more to the side of their flagship.

Lord Howard was as surprised as anyone to find so little of the Armada to attack. Moreover, he could see the floundering *San Lorenzo*, a tempting prize for the Lord Admiral. Abruptly changing his plans, he gave Drake the honour of leading the squadrons of the English fleet against the *San Martin* and took his own squadron towards the *San Lorenzo* which, unable to steer, ran aground near Calais and keeled right over towards the land, her guns pointing harmlessly into the air. Howard could not take his larger ships into such shallow water so he sent in smaller boats for the kill, and a fierce fight developed until Hugh de Moncada was shot through the head with a musket-ball. Then the English swarmed all over the galleass, stripping her of everything of value until frightened off by warning cannon-shots from Calais, as the Governor made it clear that he wanted his share of the spoils.

The attack on the *San Lorenzo*, if understandable, was also a grave mistake. Fifty Englishmen were killed, and English casualties in this one action amounted to something like half their losses in the entire campaign. And for something like an hour the fleet was deprived of some of its finest ships at the moment when the Spaniards were at their most vulnerable.

Meanwhile, Drake had led his squadron towards the *San Martin*. Closer and closer he came. Ammunition on both sides was now desperately low and precious shot could not be wasted at long range. At perhaps 100 yards he opened fire, followed in turn by the other ships in line ahead which received their answering thunders from the Spanish flagship. After Drake, came Frobisher in his *Triumph* and Hawkins in his *Victory*. Incredibly, in those early hours of Monday morning the Spaniards not only survived the English broadsides, but managed to re-form a depleted version of their once majestic crescent. Gradually, some of the greatest of the Armada's ships returned – some twenty-five of them – the galleons of Portugal and Castile, two or three of the Biscayans including the giant *Grangrin*, and the flagships of de Leyva, Bertendona, and Oquendo. But by now the advantages were all with the English who had numerical superiority, better seamanship, fresher supplies, and better ships which had sustained practically no damage. The Spanish ships suffered severely. Their decks were crowded with soldiers and littered with the dead and dying. Desperately their crews tried to pump out water flooding in from the gaping holes which were appearing near the waterline in many of the ships. Some Spanish ships were by now sitting targets, their guns silent, their ammunition spent. It seemed that they would be totally destroyed.

Suddenly, there was a fierce squall which interrupted the battle for about twenty minutes. When it had subsided the Spaniards, unbelievably, began to re-form, offering once more to do battle with their adversaries. But this time the English held off. They, too, had run out of ammunition and that day both Howard and Drake sent messages to the coast urging more powder and shot to finish the job they were doing so well.

For the Spaniards there was no one to write to, and time was running out. All the first-line ships had sustained grievous damage and considerable loss of life. During Monday's squall one of the great Biscayans, *Maria Juan*, sank, and during the night the *San Mateo* and *San Felipe*, both leaking badly, ran aground and were taken by the Dutch. Meanwhile, the wind rose and on Monday night the Armada moved before it up the Channel, followed all the time by the watch-dog fleet of the English. The Spaniards were not to know that the English guns were empty and that even now, had they attempted a landing, the English fleet could have done practically nothing about it. The following morning the Spaniards found themselves near the

Knave ♥

The Pope Consulting with his Cardinalls & Contributing a Million of Gold towards the Charge of the Armada.

VIII ♦

The L.ᵈ Hen: Seymor wᵗʰ 40 English and Dutch Ships keeping the Coast of the Netherlands to hinder yᵉ Prince of Parma's coming forth.

VII ♦

The Army of 20000 Souldiers laid along yᵉ Southern Coast of England.

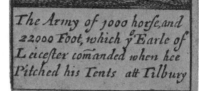

King ♥

The Army of 1000 horse, and 22000 Foot, which yᵉ Earle of Leicester comanded when hee Pitched his Tents att Tilbury.

IX ♠

Spanish Comander taken prisoners & brought into England.

VIII ♠

The Spanish Ships lost on the Coast of Scotland and 700 Souldiers and Marriners cast a Shoare.

III ♠

Queene Eliz: wᵗʰ Nobles and Gentry and a great number of people giving God humble thanks in St Pauls Church and having set upp the Ensignes taken from the Spaniards.

IIII ♠

Queene Eliz Riding in Triumph through London in a Chariot drawn by two Horses and all yᵉ Companies attending her wᵗʰ their Baners.

sands of Zeeland – too near. In a moment it seemed the Armada must run itself aground and be smashed to pieces more certainly than by any cannon. Then, within literally minutes of catastrophe, the wind backed completely, and the Spaniards were able to move out into deeper water.

The English were disgusted, the Spanish ecstatic at such fortune. It was an omen that God, after all, had not deserted them. But in truth there was nothing now that the Spaniards could do to reverse the disasters that had befallen them. All that day they passed up the North Sea chased by the English and in the evening they held a Council of War. They decided that if the wind changed, they would try to beat their way back through the Channel and still carry out their mission. But the wind did not change and so they had no choice but to continue up past Scotland and strike a long and hazardous course back to Spain. For four days the English kept their company past Hull, past Berwick, and then, on 12 August the English fleet, having seen their enemies safely off the premises, headed for the Firth of Forth.

The Armada destroyed

It was some six days later that the English ships arrived back at the ports near the Thames, coinciding with a display of pomp and pageantry unparalleled elsewhere in Elizabeth's reign. For on 18 August and again on the 19th the Queen inspected her troops in their camp at Tilbury. There were probably not more than 10,000 of them, certainly not enough to have stopped Parma's veterans had they been able to land. And their commander, the Earl of Leicester, was certainly no military genius. But they represented the patriotism of England, and as such it was in some ways the climax of the reign. In the words of Garrett Mattingly:

'Perhaps an objective observer would have seen no more than a battered, rather scraggy spinster in her middle fifties perched on a fat white horse, her teeth black, her red wig slightly askew, dangling a toy sword, and wearing an absurd little piece of parade-armour like something out of a theatrical property-box. But that was not what her subjects saw, dazzled as they were by more than the sun on the silver breastplate or the moisture in their eyes. They saw Judith and Esther, Gloriana and Belphoebe, Diana the virgin huntress and Minerva the wise protectress, and best of all their own beloved Queen and Mistress, come in this hour of danger in all simplicity to trust herself among them. The

touching rightness of the gesture whipped them to a pitch of enthusiasm which could find expression only in a wild babel of shouted blessings, endearments, and protests of devotion.'

The Queen chose this moment to make what was perhaps her greatest speech – perhaps the greatest speech by any English sovereign:

'My loving people, we have been persuaded by some that are careful for our safety, to take heed how we commit ourselves to armed multitudes, for fear of treachery. But I assure you, I do not desire to live in distrust, my faithful and loving people. Let tyrants fear. I have always so behaved myself that, under God, I have placed my chiefest strength and safeguard in the loyal hearts and good will of my subjects; and therefore I am come amongst you as you see, at this time, not for my recreation and disport, but being resolved, in the midst and heat of the battle, to live or die amongst you all, and to lay down for my God and for my kingdom and for my people, my honour and my blood, even in the dust. I know I have the body of a weak and feeble woman, but I have the heart and stomach of a king, and of a king of England too, and think foul scorn that Parma or Spain, or any prince of Europe should dare to invade the borders of my realm; to which, rather than any dishonour shall grow by me, I myself will take up arms, I myself will be your general, judge, and rewarder of every one of your virtues in the field. I know already for your forwardness you deserve rewards and crowns; and we do assure you, in the word of a prince, they shall be duly paid you.'

It might seem that this scene was acted a little late, seeing that the Armada had long been expelled from English waters. Yet Englishmen in August were on the whole not pleased with the performance of their navy. They still half expected Parma to make a cross-Channel dash, or the Armada to turn round and re-enter the arena. Against such contingencies, preparations were maintained for several weeks more, until it was quite clear that there would be no second coming. In these weeks people were openly critical of Howard's failure to board the great ships of the Armada and to settle the issue by the traditional methods of sea warfare.

But of course the issue had been settled in other ways. As Elizabeth was uttering her Shakespearian phrases the Spaniards were far to the north on their dreadful voyage home. Their fleet was in a desperate plight. Seven first-line ships had been lost;

To celebrate the English naval victory over the Spanish Armada in 1588, Queen Elizabeth I ordered a commemorative medal struck. The opposing fleets were shown in action, smoke belching from their guns. The Latin inscription Flavit Jehovah et dissipati sunt *(the name of God appearing in Hebrew characters) indicates how literally the outcome was attributed to divine intervention. The medal was originally struck in Holland where devout Protestants never doubted that God was on their side. Many Spaniards also derived some consolation from the knowledge that only divine disfavour had prevented them from overwhelming the enemy. Those who had actually taken part in the various engagements had fewer illusions, realizing that such mundane factors as as fire power, ship construction and naval tactics had in some measure influenced the result. Yet even Drake and his fellow officers acknowledged that the Lord had guided them to victory.*

the rest were damaged, and some were barely seaworthy. A fifth of the men were casualties; the food and water had long become little more than mould and slime. Morale, so high when the crescent entered the Channel, was fading rapidly and the first desertions had already begun.

The next weeks witnessed one of the most pitiful episodes in maritime history. In unfamiliar, cold waters, buffeted by a series of storms, the cluster of ships round Medina Sidonia dwindled. Some parted company on the long arc between the Orkneys and Shetlands down past the Hebrides towards Ireland. At least seventeen ships foundered off the Irish coast where thousands must have drowned. On one Irish beach alone 1,000 Spanish bodies were washed up. Those who staggered ashore often had their heads beaten in by the wild Irish as they lay exhausted on the sand. Among the ships lost off Ireland was the brave de Leyva's *Rata Coronada* with the full flower of Spanish chivalry among the gentlemen adventurers on board.

It was on 3 September that the *San Martin*, with Medina Sidonia delirious with fever, arrived at Santander. In the next few days, as more ships returned, the full extent of the disaster became obvious. About a half of those ships that had set out from Lisbon found their way home, and they were in a terrible condition. Many of them would never see service again and were fit only for the scrap-yard. In them men were dying in droves from starvation or disease as the ships lay in harbour, while hastily improvised hospitals were being set up at the ports. Few of Spain's great warriors survived. Pedro de Valdes was a prisoner in England; Hugh de Moncada and Alonzo de Leyva were dead; Recalde and Oquendo were both dead by November. Medina Sidonia lived on to serve Philip II and then Philip III for a further twenty years, but the memories of July and August 1588 must have haunted him to his grave.

In those days of slow communication and rapid rumour it is hardly surprising that the news of what had happened to the invincible Armada spread slowly. In the early days it was possible for people to believe what they wanted to. The Spanish Ambassador in Paris, Mendoza, had been one of the most enthusiastic organizers of the enterprise. Soon he became one of the most enthusiastic pedlars of good tidings. He wrote a carefully documented letter to Philip recounting the marvellous news that Sir Francis Drake had been captured. As late as 29 September, he wrote to the King that the Armada was refitting in the Orkneys

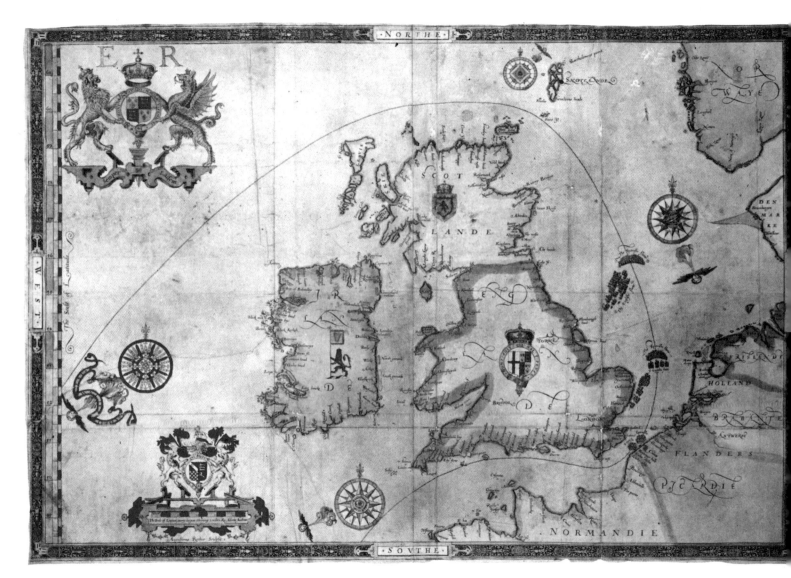

Contemporary map showing the route of the Armada. The Spanish ships had to take a long, hazardous course round the coast of Scotland back to Spain. Seventeen were wrecked off the Irish coast alone. Historians disagree on the number of ships lost and crippled beyond repair but certainly a third, maybe one half, of the Armada failed to return to Spain.

and Shetlands and would soon bear triumphantly down once more into the Channel. Philip by now knew better than his Ambassador and in the margin of the letter wrote dispiritedly: 'Nothing of this is true. It will be well to tell him so.'

The year 1588 was not the end of the Anglo-Spanish conflict. It dragged on for many years more in a desultory and rather undistinguished way: 1589 saw Drake raise an 'English Armada' in an attempt to persuade the Portuguese to support an alternative to Philip as their king. His mission was a hopeless failure. The Queen was furious and Drake did not hold another command for six years. Meanwhile, Elizabeth's struggle to frustrate Philip in the Netherlands and in France continued. In 1593 the French King, Henry IV, declared himself a Catholic and so ended Philip's hopes of installing his own candidate backed by the Catholic forces in France. In 1609 the United Provinces of the Netherlands formally won their independence from Spain, though by this time all the leading protagonists of the year of the Armada were dead.

In 1595 Drake persuaded the Queen to allow him to make an attack on the focal-point of Spanish wealth in the New World, Nombre de Dios. He was accompanied by Sir John Hawkins and the two ageing sea-dogs quarrelled incessantly from the beginning of their ill-fated voyage. Neither saw England again.

Philip, his body tormented by disease and worn out by his colossal labours, died at the Escorial in 1598, having arranged every last detail for his own funeral. And five years later his great rival, Elizabeth, followed him to the grave. Their reigns had been decisive both for the histories of their respective nations and for the world. Philip had failed to halt the tide of Reformation and to maintain the unity of his Empire. Spain's strength had been exhausted in the process and in Europe the 17th century would be dominated by France as surely as the 16th century had been dominated by Spain. But at sea England had proved herself unbeatable. That her destiny lay on the ocean could not be in doubt. The tradition of Drake and Hawkins would be followed by those who took the English flag to every corner of the globe and helped to build a great Empire and its legacy of the modern Commonwealth and world-wide community of English-speaking nations.

Index